STORIES FOR SPEAKERS AND WRITERS

Speakers and Toastmasters Library, 0-8010-8327-3

1000 Tips and Quips for Speakers and Toastmasters,
Herbert V. Prochnow, 0-8010-6895-9

A Treasury of Inspiration: Illustrations, Quotations, Poems, and Selections, Herbert V. Prochnow, 0-8010-6868-1

Stories for Speakers and Writers,
Erwin L. McDonald, 0-8010-5853-8

The Public Speaker's Handbook of Humor,
Helen and Larry Eisenberg, 0-8010-3278-4

STORIES FOR SPEAKERS AND WRITERS

A Compendium of Wit, Humor, and Inspiration from Everyday Life

by

Erwin L. McDonald

ISBN: 0-8010-5853-8

Library of Congress Catalog Card Number: 72-126559

Second printing, September 1991

Printed in the United States of America

To my grandchildren:
Rebecca
Alison
Jay-Jay

PREFACE

For the privilege of writing another book I am grateful to Baker Book House and to those who have provided a continuing market for my first book – *75 Stories and Illustrations from Everyday Life* – first published in 1964 and now available in paperback.

Stories for Speakers and Writers, like its 1964 forerunner, is a compilation of my personal experiences, featuring many stories and illustrations which, it is hoped, will prove useful to speakers, writers, and teachers, as well as inspirational and perhaps entertaining for those who read for their own edification.

That the book has a decided "country" and "Arkansas" flavor, I readily confess. As one of Alice in Wonderland's Queens would say, I could not deny that if I "tried with both hands." For it takes much more than moving to town for one born and bred in the briar patch to get away from his "raisin'."

Growing up in the backwoods of Arkansas, as I did, may not have been an enviable experience, but, dear reader, it was an experience! And while I do not go around bragging about it, neither do I apologize for it. Like Popeye, "I yam what I yam."

I have tried to give credit to those from whom I have quoted or borrowed ideas and materials. Needless to say, I am deeply grateful to all of these and to innumerable others, including overlapping categories of family, friends, and Arkansas Baptist associates, who have helped one way or another to make this book possible.

And now I hope you will get at least half as big a kick out of reading it as I have out of writing it.

– Erwin L. McDonald

CONTENTS

STORIES FOR SPEAKERS AND WRITERS

1. Now That I Am 60 . . . (Aging)

Now that I am 60, and past, I am proud of it. (Yeah, I know, I might as well be!)

One reason I am happy to be in my 60's is that a lot of the water that has "passed over the dam" can never get back up into the dam. Just for one example, second childhood should be a lark compared with adolescence!

It is quite an achievement in the world we are living in to live three score years. And those of us who have been spared for 60-plus years have a lot for which to be thankful. For one thing, we have lived through the most remarkable days in the earth's history, from horse-and-buggy days to footprints on the moon! And we are not through living yet.

Statisticians tell us that today one-fourth of all the people who have ever lived are still living. And those of us who have been around since 1907 or earlier now become a part of an ever increasing minority – those above 60.

Why is it that some people will move heaven and earth to keep their ages secret, but will break their necks to get on Social Security? The way I see it, the old saying, "Better to keep quiet and have people think you are a fool than to speak and remove all doubt," does not apply on the matter of letting your age be known. Is it not better to let people know how old you really are than to keep quiet and have them think you are five or ten years older than you are?

Recently my physician checked me over and told me that I could do anything I wanted to. Of course, in your 60's there are a lot of things you do not want to do. One of these, I have found, is mowing the lawn. But sometimes your wife puts you on the spot there. Especially is this true if you live in a neighborhood where you have a lot of eager-beaver neighbors who keep their premises spic and span.

I have reminded my wife that a lot of oldsters drop dead while working the yard. But she quotes statistics to prove that lying up in bed is a lot more dangerous than working in the yard!

The real bright spot for the Christian as the shadow of life lengthens is that he is approaching the end of life "for which the first was made." How tragic it would be to come to the end of the way without Christ as Lord and Saviour.

2. I Like You! (Attitudes)

Most of our contacts with fellow human beings are pretty incidental. The one glance we have of someone on a busy street may be the only one we will have of him on earth. But we are inclined to size one another up and decide, on meager knowledge, whom we like or dislike.

How a person walks or talks, the kind of clothes he wears, how he combs his hair – these are some of the things we consciously or unconsciously take into account in appraising people, particularly those we do not know.

Whether one is crippled or whole, fat or thin, short or tall; whether he is light or dark – these are other determinants.

If we have an opportunity to hear one speak, the language he speaks, his brogue, particularly if there is a foreign or sectional accent, also becomes a part of the picture.

When we get down to the brass tacks of the matter, will we not have to admit that we frequently put someone into his particular category of "liked" or "disliked" before we have any idea at all as to the kind of person he really is – what he believes, what he stands or falls for, what he likes or dislikes, what are his aspirations in life?

An experience in Louisville got me to thinking along this line. As I walked one morning from a restaurant back to my motel room, I met a young couple, apparently man and wife, leading a little girl. There was something quite out of the ordinary about the three that caught my attention. The man and woman, nice looking and apparently in their upper twenties, were white but the little girl, about seven, who was walking in the middle, hand-in-hand with them, was black.

I may have been staring more than I meant to be, for as I neared the people I could see there were unfriendly darts shooting out at me from the eyes of the man and the woman. I spoke to them cordially and passed on.

Quite likely this couple was used to unfriendliness from the white society because of the race of the little girl. And since I was white, they very likely thought I would naturally be a part of that unfriendliness. Yet my only feeling was one of compassion. Who the child was – whether she was Negro, Korean, Mexican, or of some other national or racial origin – made no difference at all to me. I could see that the child was being cared for out of tender love. That for me was an inspiration.

This has me wondering if much of the unfriendliness in the world may not be a defensive reaction to an imagined outside unfriendliness which frequently is not there.

3. "Mind If I Smoke?" (Bad Habits)

Some of these days when a smoker jauntily lights up a fag in close quarters with someone else who is part of a "captive audience" and says, as if he really cared, "Mind if I smoke?" that other someone is going to be one who has never had the Dale Carnegie course on how to win friends and influence people, and he is going to be truthful.

"Yes," he will say, "if it makes any difference to you, I do care!"

Then he may actually go on and preach a sermon, on some such text as, "Am I my brother's keeper?"

"I do care whether you smoke," he will say, "because I know now – as you do – from scientific proof provided by medical science, that you are increasing by at least tenfold your chances of developing lung cancer. I don't like to see anybody commit suicide, even in slow motion."

Or, if the about-to-be-saturated one is not a Christian and is thinking purely of his own likes and dislikes, he might say, perhaps with a sprinkling of strong words, "Yes, my friend, I do care whether you smoke. For I do not want to inhale your fog after you. If you want to smoke and do not care if it eventually kills you, O.K.! But please wait till you are in the open, or at least out of my face!"

If you will just stand off, as one from Mars, and observe the smokers in our enlightened society, you will be amazed and at a loss to understand how intelligent adults – men and women alike – could be addicted to such a nasty, expensive, and unhealthy habit. Yet, if you ever expect to be elected to public office, you will have to have the support of "the smokers and chewers and snuff dippers" or you will never make the grade.

Would it not be something interesting to see if, instead of going around sucking on cigarettes, cigars, or pipes, grown men and women would go around sucking the same milk bottles they were on as infants? Well, this would be a far more healthful habit than smoking. And it could be done without adding to the problem of air pollution for any nearby persons who had been weaned and no longer suck even so much as their thumbs, let alone cancer sticks.

"Mind if I smoke?"

No, go right ahead, brother! I am already burning up!

4. Read the Book! (Bible)

Life at Its Best is a book that my old friend Clabe Hankins "wouldn't give a dime for." Clabe says what he needs is a book on *Life at Its Worst.* He says he can handle life at its best.

And Clabe may have something there.

When young pastors used to cry on Professor O. W. Yates' shoulder at Ouachita College about trouble in their churches, Dr. Yates, head of the Bible department and "father confessor" for many of us, would reply in his staccato Irish brogue: "Teach a book! Teach a book!"

Dr. Yates had in mind one of any number of church study-course books always available.

As I have thought about the Yates approach to church trouble it has occurred to me that most church dissension grows out of boredom and do-nothingness. It seems to be true of church members as of people in general that "an idle mind is the devil's workshop." And just about any church study-course book a student preacher would select would suggest many things church members can and ought to be doing in their churches and in their daily lives.

Dr. Yates would not have thought of teaching a book as an end in itself. But the mere fact that the pastor of a church with its troubles would lead his people to vote to study a book would be a positive achievement.

Dorothy Canfield Fisher has said: "Through books . . . ideas find their way to human brains, and ideals to human hearts and souls."

The skeptics might retort: "Yeh, through what books and ideas and what human brains, and what human hearts and souls?"

Would we not have to confess that most of us Christians today feed our minds and our souls a lot more on the daily news than we do on the eternal verities found in the Bible – the Book of Books?

To be sure we need to keep up with what is going on the world over. But if all we do is to center on the tragedy that spotlights the news, we become "of all men most miserable." We need to read our Bibles to give us balance and sense of perspective.

5. Willingly Blind (Blindness)

As I drove across northeast Arkansas on a recent Sunday morning, I saw an elderly man feeling his way, by cane, along the main street of a small town. His eyes were wide open, but it was obvious that he could not see.

Most of us will never know what it is like to be blind. But each of us can get a slight idea as to what it is like, through a very simple experiment. If you would like to do something to help your imagination, close your eyes and keep them closed for several minutes while you meditate:

"This is what it is like to be blind. A blind person cannot see where and how to walk. He can tell little difference, if any, between daylight and dark.... He can hear the mockingbird running through its repertoire in the bushes, but he cannot see this little vocalist.... He can hear the lawnmower running, but he cannot see the clean, green carpet back of the mower.... He can hold his loved ones in his arms, but he cannot see their faces.... And on and on for the rest of life!"

This is just a slight exposure to what it is like to be blind. Now let us make an application or two in other realms.

Whether or not you insist that our government is a republic and not a democracy, you will have to agree that under this government people of all classes have more freedom and more opportunities than people have under any other government on earth. Yet, a lot of our people spend their time running the government down as if it were something alien and something aimed at the downfall and enslavement of us all. This in spite of the fact that the government is us; its officials are our people, elected by us; and its laws are made and enforced or unenforced, revised or unrevised, annulled or not annulled, by us. In our government, the government is us!

So, in the church. The church is us – those of us who have professed faith in Christ and have followed him in baptism into church membership, openly accepting his Great

Commission as our world commission. Yet, how many church members there are who live in unholy isolation and speak of the church as "they"!

You would call a man crazy who had good eyes but would not use them — one who would insist on keeping his eyes shut while he went stumbling along without seeing. But how different would a man like this be from those who insist on shutting their eyes to the blessings and opportunities that are theirs as Americans and as Christians?

6. Not "Tired Blood" (Boredom)

Contrary to the TV commercials, "that tired feeling" may be due to any number of things other than "tired blood."

An old book that I picked up at a used book store has some pointed suggestions. The book is *Two Lifetimes in One,* by Marie Beynon Ray, published by Bobbs Merrill in 1940.

Author Ray does not deal with the "tired blood" theory of tiredness, but she has much to say about what causes and what does not cause tiredness. As the title of her book implies, one way to make whatever years one has in this vale of tears count for the most is to learn to cope with fatigue. For one who is "dead tired" a big part of each twenty-four hours is for all practical purposes dead while still living.

It is the conclusion of Mrs. Ray that anyone in average good health need not go on being worn out all of the time.

What do you suppose this book suggests as the No. 1 enemy, in this matter of chronic fatigue? Overwork? No. All of the tests and surveys reported here — and there are many — indicate that work itself, particularly work requiring mental exertion, is not what tires. The No. 1 enemy is boredom!

And here are the other prime causes of tiredness listed in order of their importance: worry — a real killer; a sense of inferiority; fear — which often brings sudden death to those who have nothing else wrong with them; indecision — what a curse for one not to be able to make sensible decisions and stand by them; oversensitivity or overemotionalism; and, finally, pusillanimity, or a lack of "that good sort of stoicism necessary to the struggle of life."

Mrs. Ray has a chapter entitled "God Helps Those Who Help Themselves," immediately followed by such other chapters as "So Help Yourself!," "Balance Your Life," "Behave Yourself!," "What Do You Do Between 5 P.M. and 11 P.M.?," and "Your Secret Sin."

This book has a lot of truth and down-to-earth good suggestions. But when we get to dealing with such handicaps as boredom, worry, and all of the other life wreckers, we need the remarkable resources of God available to us through Christ.

7. All Are Brothers (Brotherhood)

Several years ago, while driving across the state of Kentucky, I came unexpectedly upon a large crowd of people standing at the end of a bridge which towered above a mountain river. They were packed close together and were staring in silent awe into the river far below.

A man had missed the bridge and had plunged in his car to his death in the river.

There was something in the solemnity of the occasion that made me realize at once that this was not just something that had happened to one man. It had happened to this awestruck crowd. And it had happened to me.

It was obvious to me, as a late-comer to the group of onlookers, that there was a common tie that bound us all together in the experience of death. One of our fellow creatures had suddenly gone on that mysterious journey to the Great Beyond, a journey that each and every one of us would be going on sooner or later.

As the import of the experience hit me, I noticed something remarkable about the crowd. It was neither white nor black, rich nor poor, cultured nor uncultured, though it was all of these. It was humanity. No one was thinking about color or creed or social status. At a time like this the people were just fellow human beings, drawn together in their compassion for the one who had died.

I never knew anything about the man who had died. To this day I do not know whether he was "Jew or Gentile, barbarian or Greek, bond or free." As far as I know, I never met him in life. But in his death I feel that I lost a brother – at least a potential brother.

Whether we like it or not, all men are brothers in creation. Each one, as Adam the first man, God has created to be in his own image.

More than two hundred years ago a Mr. Woolman, who was a pioneer in the movement to abolish slavery, wrote:

"When we remember that all nations are one Blood... that in this World we are but Sojourners, that we are subject to the like Afflictions and Infirmities of Body, and like Disorders and Frailties in Mind, the like Temptations, the same Death, the same Judgment, and that the Alwise Being is Judge and Lord over us all, it seems to raise an Idea of a general Brotherhood, and a Disposition easy to be touched with a Feeling of each other's Afflictions."

8. Freeway Squatting (Change)

One of life's big handicaps for many today is not being able to take the freeway access lanes in stride.

There are still a lot of people who seem to think that the access lanes were made for motorists to squat in. Instead of going ahead and using the lanes to keep moving in until they can work their way onto the main highway, many a driver stops as soon as he has started onto the access lane, hazarding his own life and the lives of others as he sits – as a sitting duck – and waits till he can cut all the way across the access lane and into his favorite lane of the main highway.

Wasn't it Burns who said:

> "O wad some power the giftie gie
> the squatting motorists
> To see themselves as drivers
> back of them see them"?

There is nothing particularly disgraceful about having learned to drive in the horse-and-buggy days – unless one insists on driving in this jet-propulsion age just the way he drove in those days of yore.

All of which points up the dire necessity of being able to adjust to a swiftly changing world. How many a business has gone bankrupt because its operators insisted not only on doing business at the same old stand, but in the same old way? (And let us not forget that, in this regard, our churches are businesses!)

One of my fellow preachers was musing the other day on the earth-shaking changes that are taking place all around us every day.

"I am not longing to be retired," he said, "but, quite frankly, I am glad that I will be stepping down in another ten or twelve years. I must admit that I simply cannot adjust to the changes that have already happened and are in prospect in the immediate future. I am just not capable of being re-tooled for the new age."

Some can adjust to change, taking the tides in their affairs as that which "leads on to fortune." But those who cannot or will not change are likely to find "all the voyage of their life" to be "bound in shallows, and in miseries."

An example of one left high and dry in the new age is the young theologian who said that he was not interested in depth study to determine from the original languages what the Scriptures really say – he just wanted "something I can believe"!

9. Winning Children (Children)

Helping children to make the right decisions is a lot different from making the decisions for them, as everyone who has ever been a child or a parent knows. And reaching right decisions involves right thinking.

The child who for any reason grows up without developing the practice of straight, hard thinking is poorly equipped both for this life and for the life to come.

Why is it that so many parents become disturbed over the decisions of their children to accept Christ as their Lord and Savior and to follow him in baptism and into a place of growth and service in the church?

It is right that parents should want their children to be sure in making this all-important decision. But many well-meaning parents actually let their concern at this point become road blocks in the spiritual lives of their little ones.

There used to be a pretty general feeling among parents of another generation that the age of twelve was, for some mystical reason, the "age of accountability" for children and that none of them should try to decide what they will do about accepting Christ until they have attained this age.

My father was one who believed this. He used to invite adults into our home to reason with them from the Scriptures, thus leading many of them to accept Christ. But when I asked him to help me, he replied, "Son, when you are older." But my father died when I was eleven and it was not till I was 18 that I became a Christian.

I agree with a young pastor who said to me, "The logical ones to win the children are their Christian parents." He said that he used to rush in on the invitation of parents to win the children. Now he counsels with the parents and tries to help them to see that this is a great and wonderful privilege that should be theirs.

"Let the redeemed of the Lord say so" (Ps. 107:2) is not only a call for all Christians to witness to the glory and majesty of their Redeemer. It is particularly a call to parents to witness to their own children.

10. Christmas Is Love (Christmas)

One of my favorite Christmas stories is that of the visit of the Magi to the crib of the baby Jesus, a story found in Matthew 2.

Because three gifts are mentioned as given by the wise men, it has been concluded by some that there were three of the Magi. Literature has not only numbered the men but has named them and attached them to their respective gifts: Casper with his gold; Melchoir with his frankincense; and Balthazzar with his myrrh. And the hymn "We Three Kings of Orient Are" fills in the details with which legend has adorned the story.

Apparently no symbolism is intended by the Scriptures to be attached to the gifts. But since gold, as a precious metal, was used in worship; frankincense, in perfume; and myrrh in medicine and embalming, these objects were worthy of offering to royalty. Their presentation to the Christ by the Magi indicated a great depth of honor and adoration. The wise men gave of their best to the Lord.

The Magi apparently believed that a star could be the counterpart or angel of a great man, as they followed the Bethlehem star to Jesus' crib.

The greatest thing about the Magi was their love for the Christ. Their long and perhaps perilous trip and their sacrificial gifts worthy of a king would have been as "sounding brass or a tinkling cymbol" but for this love.

In the demonstration of their great love, the Magi "being dead yet speak." Their story continues to warm human hearts and to remind that we can never sink so low in our inhumanity to one another as to break out of the orb of God's love to us through Jesus Christ.

The story of the Magi, states *The Interpreter's Bible*

(Vol. 7, p. 256), "expresses the truth that men have been brought from far and by many ways to worship Christ. It also breathes the sense of wonder and thanksgiving that through the birth of this Child, and his subsequent life, death, and resurrection, the world has been redeemed."

Christmas is a good time to be reminded that Christ, who gave himself a ransom for every one of us, has charged: "If you love me, keep my commandments," and that one of those commandments is, "Love one another."

11. "Forgive Christmasses" (Christmas)

A little girl who had been counting the days till Christmas could not help but be puzzled by what the day before Christmas was like, reports *Gospel Herald.*

On Christmas eve she had noticed:

Dad seemed to be loaded down with worries as well as bundles. Mom's anxiety had reached the breaking point several times during the day.

Anywhere the little girl went, she seemed to be in the way more than usual. There was such a hustle and bustle by so many to do so much, all in the name of being "ready for Christmas."

By the time the child was hustled off to bed, the feverish planning for Christmas had completely unnerved her. So, as she knelt to pray the Lord's Prayer, she got part of it mixed up and prayed: "Forgive us our Christmases as we forgive those who Christmas against us."

Has Christmas in our day actually become a load for us rather than a lift?

In a small town just before Christmas I saw a poor family trying to do what it expected of itself on a Christmas shopping trip. There were three of them — Dad, Mother, and teen-age daughter. It was obvious at a glance that Christmas was an extra financial burden for them.

The day was cold. While mother and daughter were comfortably dressed, their apparel showed considerable age and wear. Dad wore overalls and two shirts, but no jacket or coat. As he walked his body seemed to be trying to nestle in itself, much as cattle left unprotected in winter blasts. His only mark of self-respect (?) was a half-smoked cigarette hanging jauntily between his lips as he walked with hands in pockets. He seemed to be somewhat of a lamb being led to the slaughter.

The name of this family is Legion, for there are many like them.

Perhaps we need to go back to Bethlehem and look again at the first Christmas.

Free of the burdens of Christmas as we have them today and with their eyes and hearts fixed on Jesus, the shepherds, poor though they were, became possessed of the true spirit of Christmas. Luke reports that they "... made known abroad the saying which was told them concerning this child..." and "...returned, glorifying and praising God for all the things that they had heard and seen, as it was told unto them."

12. Not in a Manger (Christmas)

In Revell's *Book of Illustrations* for the Sunday School Lessons of 1964 is a true story of something that happened a long time ago in the life of a Skid Row resident and a little orphan boy.

The day before Christmas, a Skid Row alcoholic found a dollar bill. Greatly excited at his good fortune, he began trying to decide how to spend the money. Finally, he decided he would go to his favorite saloon and treat some of his friends to a drink.

But on the way to the saloon, the old tramp passed a sporting goods store and espied a baseball bat in the window. This brought back haunting memories of long ago, when he had been a poor boy who longed to play ball but who was never able to own a bat.

Seeing that the bat was priced at only a dollar, the old man went in and bought it. Then he took it to an orphanage, just down the street. Placing it in the doorway, he rang the doorbell and ran away.

Finding the bat, the keeper of the orphanage made a Christmas present of it for an awkward, gangly boy who liked to play ball but who up to this time had never owned a bat. The boy grew up to become a famous man – Babe Ruth, the home-run king.

Would it not have been wonderful if the old man could have known what that dollar bat would mean in the hands of the lowly orphan boy?

There is no way of assessing little gifts and little kindnesses.

Sometimes the last days just before Christmas become so cluttered with frenzied activities and shopping sprees that we lose our perspective.

The Christmas spirit nevertheless for a little while helps us to forget ourselves and remember others. And as we show our love for others, a wonderful feeling of joy comes to us. Christ is born again – in our hearts.

13. Habit or Experience (Churchgoing)

Most churches are emptied in nothing flat immediately after the last "amen." So a Florida pastor had his curiosity more than gently stirred one Sunday morning recently when he saw a young couple rushing into the church auditorium after the service, instead of hurrying to get out.

He noticed that the young lady was frantically searching for something among the pews. Thinking that she had surely lost something of great value, he offered his assistance. But, to his surprise, the search ended when the girl found a copy of the order of service for the day.

"With a smile of relief," reported the pastor, "the young

lady accepted the outstretched hand of her boy-friend and they left."

The pastor allows that he did not need to be "a detective or the son of a detective" to solve the mystery. Here was a girl who had left home that morning ostensibly to attend church but had spent her time somewhere else. She needed the order of service to keep her tracks covered.

But the pastor was philosophic about it, though justifiably pointed, as revealed later in his "Pastor's Paragraphs" of the church bulletin. Wrote the pastor:

"I have thought about this incident several times recently. What proof do we have that we have been to church? Is a piece of paper the best we can do? It may be an order of service, or certificate of church membership, or a baptismal certificate – so what! These things may serve as positive proof for some but in the eyes of our Lord, they prove little or nothing.

"Our Lord is not concerned about an order of service, but the order of our lives. No one had to ask Peter and John if they had been to church. Their godly lives served as proof positive (Acts 4:13)."

And then, for the special benefit of his own flock, the pastor wrote: "I'll look forward to seeing you Sunday – before, during, and after the service."

Going to church can be just a habit. When it is that, it is a bad habit. For then it becomes pure hypocrisy.

Going to church at its best involves far more than being physically present in a church service. It means being personally involved in a worship service – talking to God out of the heart, but also earnestly listening for God's direction.

The big question after church is not, "How did the preacher do?" but "How did I do as a church attender and worshipper?"

14. Supermarket Churches? (Church Mission)

The idea of churches as supermarkets where pre-packaged religion is to be had on a "take it or leave it" basis had not occurred to me till I read something from Paul Oestreicher. Said Mr. Oestreicher:

"We continue to be mainly concerned with religion instead of with human beings. The way in which we spend our money and deploy our human resources is proof enough, if proof were needed. As institutions, all our churches spend the greater part of their wealth – and I mean wealth – in employing clergymen and maintaining religious buildings.

"What is mildly amusing is that we express surprise that the majority of people seem to feel no need for what we offer and even less need for the places in which we offer it."

And here is the projection of the supermarket image:

"We can now offer the Christian religion in a variety of more or less modernized packages and we do it on the basis of "take it or leave it."

"Most men prefer to leave it, some of them not because they reject Christ, but because we bear so little resemblance to him."

There are lots of different ideas on how to measure the greatness or success of a church. As Mr. Oestreicher emphasizes here, success for a church entails much more than building and staffs and budgets.

An Episcopal bishop – Paul Moore, Jr., of Washington, D.C. – gave much food for thought when he was interviewed recently by Louis Cassels of United Press International:

"The most important mission of a church," said Bishop Moore, "is to present to the world a true image of Jesus Christ. If a congregation's life is such that outsiders can see Christ reflected in it, then it is doing its job, no matter whether it's large or small, rich or poor, famous or obscure."

Pressed for more details, Bishop Moore said:

"The kind of love which is a sign of Christ is willing to

share suffering, to accept each other's failings. It's a kind of love you can almost feel when you are among people who have it. And it's infectious. People who enter the circle of it want to stay and be part of it, even when they don't understand where it's coming from."

Seen much of that kind of love lately?

More to the point, are you and I helping to kindle any of this kind of love in our own churches?

15. Modern Prodigal (Compassion)

In the dramatic parable of the prodigal son as told by the Lord in Luke 15, the prodigal "gathered all together and took his journey into a far country and there wasted his substance with riotous living." But a modern prodigal, of whom we have read in the papers lately, has demonstrated that one can live riotously without ever leaving the parental premises.

Taking advantage of the absence from home of his family on vacation, an 18-year-old Detroit high school dropout staged a beer party in the back yard at his home.

The party got out of hand when police came to quiet it down and three policemen were injured and fourteen youth arrested before it was over.

Sobered by a 15-day jail sentence and a $100 fine, the party host commented: "I would rather have served three months in jail than have smeared my father's name all over town."

The father, embittered by a long succession of misbehavior on the part of his son, said: "I disown him completely. I wouldn't pay five cents to get him out."

As the father packed the son's clothes into two cardboard boxes to be handed to him with his "walking orders" when he should complete the jail sentence, he said, "I've been through hell because of that boy. I can't take any more from him. He is a hoodlum."

According to the father, the youth had been a model son until he was 15. Then he had started rebelling against the authority of his father and of his teachers.

"He was brought up decently," the father recalled. "He attended church every Sunday until he was 15. Teachers said he was intelligent. They said he had a high IQ. But something went wrong. Somehow I must have failed. The burden is mine. I'd be wrong to say somebody else is to blame. I'm his father. I have to assume the blame."

That was the story one day. But in the papers the next day the story took a happier turn. On learning that his son had repented, the father changed his mind and said he would take the boy back and give him another chance — once he had served the jail sentence.

There was no mention of clothing this prodigal in "the best robe," or of "putting a ring on his hand and shoes on his feet" and of killing the fatted calf. But the father said: "I will let this be just a memory."

Said the sobered teen-ager from his jail cell: "I've got about the best old man in the world."

16. Real Christians (Discipleship)

"Real Christians are a lot alike, regardless of their denomination."

These words spoken by a layman have stuck with me.

Who is a real Christian? I did not ask my friend to elaborate. But knowing him as I do, I believe he would expect the following to be true of a "real" Christian regardless of denominational tag:

A real Christian has repented of his sins, has trusted Christ as his Savior, and has yielded himself to Christ as the Lord of his life.

A real Christian follows his Lord in baptism and into the fellowship of the church of his choice. He loves the church as he loves his Lord and gives himself for it.

A real Christian loves God and loves people. Not only does he love those who love him, but, with the help of the Lord, he loves even the unlovable, having a real compassion for the rankest of sinners.

A real Christian is not a fair-weather Christian. He is conscious of God's purpose for his life and his presence with him. Through sunshine and shadow he looks to God for his strength and his direction. He is a man of prayer and a student of God's Word.

A real Christian's heart is touched by the suffering and needs of others. He opens his heart and his purse to help others.

A real Christian knows that God is no respector of persons and he has love and respect for people of all nations, of all races, of all classes. He neither looks up to any man nor down on any.

A real Christian does not return evil for evil, but good for evil. He is long-suffering and kind. He remembers that Christ prayed even for those who crucified him: "Father, forgive them; they know not what they do."

A real Christian does not run off at the mouth. With the help of the Lord he keeps his tongue in due bounds. So he is no backbiter, no talebearer.

A real Christian recognizes God as "the giver of every good and perfect gift." He is truly grateful to the Lord for blessings both material and spiritual. He endeavors to be a good steward of all of his blessings. He is not stingy. He knows that it really is "more blessed to give than to receive."

A real Christian is not ashamed of what the Lord has done for him. He gladly bears a witness and tries prayerfully and earnestly to bring others within the circle of God's saving grace through Christ. Yes, *real* Christians are a lot alike. But they are not like a lot of nominal church members, regardless of the denomination.

17. Of Mules and Men (Discipline)

There sometimes appears in the best of us a streak of mulishness. So suggests Preacher W. B. O'Neal of Gravel Ridge.

What Paul said about "keeping under" his body and bringing it "into subjection" (I Cor. 9:27) got Preacher O'Neal to recalling what he has noticed about mules:

"A mule is brought under and kept in subjection. But he still has a disposition to kick, to paw, to buck, to snort, to shy and to shun harness.

"A mule is kept under with bit and rein of control. Once he is harnessed and geared for service, he is commanded to get up, to gee, to haw, and, at the proper time, to whoa. He is lashed, if he is disobedient (Ps. 89:30-33).

"You can cause a mule to like you by gentle treatment, by supplying him with eats, by currying and petting. Of necessity you must see that he is properly shod, but your greatest task is that of educating him to walk where he ought to walk, whether it be to follow a furrow or to stay on a ridge.

"When a mule gets old, he may be retired and kept well because of the service he has rendered, but even then, he may kick. Some do."

And speaking of kicking mules, there are just two places of safety with relation to mule hindquarters – points well out of range or points close, close to the mule's warm side. And the same applies to one's relations with people streaked with mulishness.

So, if you detect that some of your friends are avoiding you, or staying closer to you than you could wish, you might go through a clinic somewhere and have a test for mulishness. Sometimes even your best friends won't tell you.

It was hard to tell, when some of us were growing up, down on Bunker, who was working for whom. The mules were supposed to be "work stock," but some of us spent a big part of our most formative years catering to their needs

– or trying to get them into positions of catering to ours.

You had to water them and feed them and harness and unharness them. Once in a while you had to take them to Si Ruble's blacksmith shop and get them shod, an experience that may or may not have contributed to their sure-footedness, but which certainly increased their lethality.

We hope we will not be taken too personally as we sign off with this Scripture: "Be not as . . . the mule, which has no understanding" (Ps. 32:9).

18. "I Know You Not" (Election)

My name was not written there!

And this came as no surprise to the keeper of the book, for he had never heard of me.

But what a traumatic experience it was for me!

There I was in Memphis, on the last leg of a round-trip from Little Rock to New York, and the agent for the air line to which I was supposed to transfer neither had a reservation for me nor a spare seat. And all of my immediate plans had been constructed – like a cob house, I could see now – around getting back to Little Rock on that plane that was scheduled to leave within an hour.

If I did not catch that plane, I would not get to check in at the office for some urgent work before having to leave for still another away-from-home engagement.

The station manager was obviously real disturbed by now, for there was nothing wrong with my ticket. It was the other line's fault, he told me, concluding that the company with whom the ticket and the journey had originated had failed to clear the last lap of the trip with the connecting feeder line. But he assured me that he would do everything he could to make a place for me. I was to sit in the lobby and listen for him to page me.

A scant thirty minutes before flight time, I saw the manager reach for his microphone. Did he have my problem worked out and was he about to call me?

No such luck. Instead, I heard him paging a friend of mine.

All at once the facts of the situation dawned on me. My friend had been my traveling companion on the trip and originally had been ticketed to travel back with me. But he had changed his departure to a later date. Evidently, when he had arranged for his ticket to be changed, the airline had made the mistake of cancelling me out and leaving him on the book for an all-important one and only seat on the next flight from Memphis to Little Rock.

A hop, skip, and a jump, and I had cancelled out my friend and had gotten old No. 1 a seat.

If it is so upsetting to miss one flight of a plane trip down here below, imagine what a shocking experience it would be to appear before God on the Great Judgment Day only to discover that one's name is not found in the Lamb's Book of Life.

19. Going on a Trip (Eternity)

"I'm getting ready to make a trip," my middle-aged friend said to me as I visited him in his hospital room.

"Where are you going?" I asked.

"I don't know," he said, "for I have never been there before."

This was the first indication I had that my friend knew, as his family and friends had known for sometime, that he could not recover from his illness. The doctors had told us that he had cancer, but they had not told him.

In a few weeks this friend, a beloved schoolteacher who had helped many of us impecunious youths to go to school, slipped away to "that land from whose bourne no traveler returns."

Each one of us is getting ready to make such a trip. And

while we do not know much about what the place is like to which we Christians go, God has given us some glimpses.

From Revelation 7:16-17 we learn that in the blessed place called heaven those who arrive "shall hunger no more, neither thirst any more; neither shall the sun light on them, nor any heat. For the Lamb which is in the midst of the throne shall feed them, and shall lead them unto living fountains of waters: and God shall wipe away all tears from their eyes."

Permit me to quote, now, from *Bible Study for Married Young People*:

"A young man in the military service in South Vietnam, enduring the hardships and dangers of jungle warfare, looked forward to the completion of his overseas assignment and his return to the love and comfort of his American home. Is this not a parable of the battle of life as we look forward to our place among the redeemed in glory? We are helped to endure the heartaches and pain of the moment by reflecting on what awaits us."

The great difference between the Christian and the non-Christian is not that the Christian finds life easy and free of heartache and the non-Christian always has it rough. Rather, it is that the Christian has the assurance that "the sufferings of this present time are not worthy to be compared with the glory which shall be revealed in us" (Rom. 8:18).

As the patriarch Abraham, we look "forward to the city which has foundations, whose builder and maker is God" (Heb. 11:10, RSV).

20. Song in the Night (Faith)

Some of the greatest of our Christian hymns have been written out of hearts in deepest sorrow. A striking example is the well-known and widely-loved "It Is Well with My Soul."

As a special treat to his wife and their four children, Chicago businessman H. G. Spafford gave them a trip to Europe. Mrs. Spafford and the children sailed from New York in November 1873, aboard the French luxury liner "S.S. Ville du Havre."

All was pleasant sailing for the first several days. But at 2 a.m. on November 22, while sailing on quiet waters, the liner was acccidentally rammed by the British iron sailing boat "Lochearn."

Within two hours of the tragedy, the ship settled to the bottom of the Atlantic, taking with it 226 persons, among them the four Spafford children. Nine days later, Mrs. Spafford cabled her husband from Cardiff, Wales: "Saved alone." Her husband's immediate reply was: "I am so glad to trust the Lord when it will cost me something."

As soon as he could, Mr. Spafford booked passage on another ship and was soon crossing the Atlantic to join his grief-stricken wife. On the way over – according to the account carried in Ernest K. Emurian's book, *Sing the Wondrous Story,* Spafford was told by the captain of the ship when they were over the waters where the Ville du Havre had gone down.

Unable to sleep that night, but sustained in his sorrow by a great faith, the father composed what was to become the popular hymn:

When peace, like a river, attendeth my way,
When sorrows like sea billows roll;
Whatever my lot, Thou hast taught me to say,
It is well, it is well with my soul.

Though Satan should buffet, tho' trials should come,
Let this blest assurance control,
That Christ has regarded my helpless estate,
And hath shed his own Blood for my soul.

My sin – oh, the bliss of this glorious tho't:
My sin not in part, but the whole
Is nail'd to the cross and I bear it no more,
Praise the Lord, praise the Lord, O my soul.

And, Lord, haste the day when the faith shall be sight,
The clouds be roll'd back as a scroll,
The trump shall resound and the Lord shall descend,
Even so, it is well with my soul.

21. Meaning of Independence (Fourth of July)

July has been described as "the most important month in American history."

Three historic events of great significance, which occurred in July, were:

The adoption of the Declaration of Independence – on July 4, 1776 – by the Continental Congress;

The Battle of Gettysburg, which marked the turning point in the Civil War; and

Ratification of the Fourteenth Amendment to the Constitution of the United States, granting to all persons born or naturalized in the United States equal protection under the law and forbidding the states to deprive any person of "life, liberty or property without due process of law."

Of course, the first of these stands as the high-water mark of American history.

In a campaign speech in 1858, Abraham Lincoln said of the Declaration of Independence and those who produced it:

"They grasped not only the whole race of men then living, but they reached forward and seized upon the farthest posterity: they erected a beacon to guide their children and their children's children, and the countless myriads who should inhabit the earth in other ages.

"Wise statesmen as they were, they knew the tendency of posterity to breed tyrants; and so they established these great self-evident truths, that when in the distant future, some men, some faction, some interest, should set up the doctrine that none but rich men, or none but white men, or none but Anglo Saxons, were entitled to life, liberty, and the pursuit of happiness, their posterity might look up again to the Declaration of Independence and take courage to renew the battle which their fathers began – so that truth, and justice, and mercy, and all the humane and Christian virtues might not be extinguished from the land; so that no man hereafter would dare to limit and circumscribe the great principles on which the temple of liberty was being built."

In his concluding remarks, Mr. Lincoln sounded more like a preacher than a politician:

"Now, my countrymen, if you have been taught doctrines which conflict with the great landmarks of the Declaration of Independence, if you have listened to suggestions which would take from its grandeur, and mutilate the symmetry of its proportions; if you have been inclined to believe that all men are *not* created equal in those inalienable rights enumerated by our charter of liberty, let me entreat you to come back . . . to the truths that are in the Declaration of Independence."

Such reasoning is just as appropriate today as it was in 1858!

22. Real Americanism (Fourth of July)

The word *patriotism* is widely flaunted these days. But many have learned to their sorrow that it means one thing in one man's thinking and quite another in the mind of somebody else.

The dictionary *(Webster's New Collegiate)* defines patriotism as "Love of country; devotion to the welfare of one's country." But there are many today who seem to think that it is hate of one's country, at least of the Supreme Court and/or the federal government and, sometimes, Congress.

It is downright hard to tell from the ranting that certain self-styled "patriots" are doing just how they differ from any other revolutionists who stand for the overthrow, by means fair or foul, of our government.

Regardless of who they are, those who seek to impose their power and control over the lives and opinions of others and for the overthrow of our democratic processes are far from being patriots in the right sense of the word. They are dangerous, mad men who will still bear watching.

As we come to the observance of another Fourth of July, a day which certainly should have great meaning for all Americans, let us join in a new pledge of allegiance to this great land of ours.

Especially in election years, it might not be inappropriate for us to emphasize that one of the best marks of patriotism is honest and clean involvement in political affairs. Each one of us owes it to his country to do what he can to stamp out such rotten practices as stealing or buying elections. Let us stand firm against crookedness in high and low places and against the self-styled "patriots" who have warped views of Americanism.

23. Giving and Getting (Giving)

"There is no problem in giving."

So wrote Pastor Emmett F. Parks of First Baptist Church, Covina, Calif., in his church bulletin. "You only have problems when you try to get," says Pastor Parks. "You may have a problem to get kindness and warmth from another person, but isn't it wonderful that you are absolutely free to give it whether anybody else does so or not!"

This would seen to imply that you cannot make somebody love you by demanding that he do so or by blasting him because he does not, but that the way to be assured of a person's love is to love that person – putting the "give" ahead of the "get."

When someone is unkind toward me, I am really more "on the spot" than is the other person. For I must decide whether I will react and how I will react.

I can decide just to ignore the unkindness. If I can abide

in this course of action (or inaction) it may be that the other person will relent. Or he may jab back with further hostilities!

If I decide to strike back in kind, the war is on. And whether it be "cold" or "hot," wars are a lot easier to start than they are to stop.

But if I can hold onto my temper and, with the Lord's help, actually have some genuine compassion in my heart for the hostile one, perhaps I will be able to love that person, in deed and in truth. If I can, there is good prospect that the unlovable one will love back. And when that happens, there comes a tremendous change in personal relationships.

Says Joseph Parker, in commenting on I Corinthians 13:

"Where there is an abundance of love all the housekeeping goes easily, whether it be in a little cottage or a great palace or a church comprehending multitudinous of character, opinion, and force. Where there is no love there can be no reliance upon the easy working of the machinery; you may have compromise and concession, and a policy of give-and-take, but not until love rules the spirit will the life settle into rich, massive, worthy music. . . . Unless we have love everything else goes for nothing."

Lord, help us to put the "give" ahead of the "get."

24. Happen-so's (God's Providence)

One of the interesting things about life is how frequently something that happens and appears at the time to be an insignificant event turns out to be major.

As one interesting example of this, a day's travel in the wrong direction caused a young adventurer to settle in Arkansas, back in the early 1830's, instead of going on to his original destination of New Orleans. Thus Arkansas gained one of its most noted, if somewhat controversial, figures –

Albert Pike, poet, journalist, attorney, politician, school teacher, Confederate general, and Masonic executive.

Pike was returning from a trip out West on this eventful, cloudy day. With no sun in sight, he took the wrong turn, as he led a party headed for the famous Louisiana port. Not until the next day, when the sun again made its appearance, did he discover that he and his party had traveled a full day north while they had meant to be going south.

Travel-tired, Pike decided that the difference between settling in Louisiana as over against settling in Arkansas Terriory was worth something less than retracing the steps of the day's journey. So, Louisiana's loss became Arkansas' gain.

Today the restoration of the log cabin in which Pike taught school somewhere near Van Buren is located on the campus of the University of Arkansas, Fayetteville. And the spacious, two-story home Pike built in Little Rock in 1840 for what was then a fabulous sum – $7,000 – stands as the long-time residence of the David D. Terry family and a show place for persons interested in early Arkansas history.

Other landmarks of Little Rock bearing the name of this intrepid Arkansas pioneer are the Albert Pike Hotel and the Albert Pike Masonic Temple.

No one claims more space in the history of Arkansas from the early 1830's through the Civil War than this 300-pound native of the state of Massachuetts. And it all started with getting mixed up on directions in a frontier thicket.

Never take an unexpected turn of events lightly. In the providence of God it may mark a turning point in your life.

25. Freeway Troubles (God's Providence)

Did you ever wonder what you would do if your car took out on you while driving on the free-for-alls (freeways)? The fact that you occasionally see cars stopped on freeway shoulders, with lids lifted, is enough to remind you that "it could happen to you."

One day, when I was just about 30 miles and 30 minutes out of Nashville, on my way back to Little Rock, I suddenly noticed the warning light come on, on my car panel, indicating that something was going wrong and that I better see about it. A quick inspection revealed that the water was all spewed out of the radiator of my foreign-made bug.

There I was, afoot in the wide open country, with the most assurance being a sign on the opposite side of the freeway announcing a service station five miles back!

On a hunch, I started walking west, toward Memphis. Shortly a young man in a rattletrap of a car picked me up. He was having trouble, too, he said. His radiator had boiled dry. But he pushed the flivver up to 70 as we looked for a place to get help!

We found a station about four miles down the road and soon I was back in business. Apparently, the only trouble had been an accumulation of rust that had clogged the thermostat and had allowed the car to become overheated. A flushing of the radiator and refilling took care of the situation.

All of this made me grateful to the Lord on several counts. I was grateful that in the providence of God the young man who was himself in difficulty had had compassion and picked me up. Four miles would have been a long, hard hike!

I was grateful for the prompt response of the man from the service station who took time off to carry me in his truck back to the car, with a supply of water, to get the car to performing again. And when he told me how much I owed him, I was grateful that he was a reasonable man.

One thing I was especially grateful for. When I had driven my car for a hectic 40 minutes through the heart of Chicago on Superspeedway 94 the previous day, nothing had gone wrong. For on that stretch there is no place to stop.

Thank you, Lord!

26. "Thank You, Lord" (Gratitude)

A lot of us wear out our "wanters" before we have hardly turned on our "appreciators."

I cannot help wondering how many takers the Lord would have on a proposition like this: "You shall have everything you can really appreciate and be grateful for, but nothing at all for which you are not appreciative and grateful."

I think most of us would need time to think that one over before saying, "It's a deal, Lord."

Some of us who have been eating two or three times as much as our bodies need to stay healthy and strong might get pretty hungry before we had another meal, under the terms of this proposition. For not even a hurried, stereotyped "We thank Thee, Lord, for this food," would necessarily turn the trick. It is mighty hard to pull the wool over the Lord's face.

Speaking of having to appreciate blessings, how many of us would have a job if we had to appreciate it or give it up?

How many of us would lose our life companions in the twinkle of an eye, for lack of appreciating them and being grateful for them?

Would America become a land without Bibles overnight?

How many church steeples would cease to be a part of the landscape if we church members had to love and appreciate our churches enough to support them, or lose them?

How many of us would suddenly become hopeless invalids, if we had to appreciate our health to keep it?

Would there be any good books left in our homes, if we lost all that we do not appreciate enough to read and heed?

How many of us would be left without roofs over our very heads if we had to lose our residences or quit deploring the fact that we cannot have bigger and fancier places to live?

Brothers and sisters, let's turn off our wanters for a few days, at least, and turn on our appreciators!

27. "Happiness Is..." (Happiness)

Many year ago I gave a relative a copy of William Lyon Phelps' little classic, *Happiness.* In the front of the book I wrote: "Keep this little book and you will always have 'Happiness' in your library. Keep the principles of the book and you will have happiness in your heart." Now I find the book back in my own library, autograph and all!

Since I am more bulging and grayer than when I gave this book, something Dr. Phelps has to say about happiness and growing old has special significance for me. (Do not go away, young readers, there is a word for you too!)

Taking note of the fact that many people become alarmed when they first discover their hair is turning gray, the noted educator says if one suddenly discovered his hair was turning green or blue, he would really have something to worry about. But, he says, when it begins to turn gray, that is just a sign "there is so much gray matter in the skull there is no longer room for it; it comes out and discolors the hair."

So, he counsels, "Don't be ashamed of your gray hair; wear it proudly, like a flag."

But there is no such thing, really, as "growing old gracefully," he says, for "old people are not graceful." Grace, he says, "belongs to youth and is its chief charm.... Young people are decorative; that is why we like them. They are slender, agile, fair, and graceful, because nobody could stand them if they were otherwise."

Just think what a horrible situation we'd face, he suggests, "if boys and girls, knowing as little as they do, were also bald, grey-headed, fat, wrinkled, and double-chinned...." Nature has so arranged things, he says, "that young people are physically attractive until they acquire some brains and sense, and are able to live by their wits; then they lose these superficial advantages. As responsibility grows, beauty and grace depart."

Even if it were possible to grow old gracefully, reasons Dr. Phelps, "it would be at best a form of resignation, a surrender; and a soldier of life should not take it lying down."

So, he concludes, "Instead of growing old gracefully, suppose we grow old eagerly, grow old triumphantly."

Thanks a million, Dr. Phelps. Anybody know somebody who would like to have half a bottle of ash blond hair dye?

28. "Cihu," Everybody! (Helpfulness)

A new word for the English language has been proposed. The word is "cihu," pronounced "ki-hoo," with emphasis on the first syllable. The word is created from the initial letters of four wrods: "Can I help you?"

First to propose the new word in Arkansas was Dr. Frank C. Laubach, the noted "Apostle to the Illiterates," on one of his visits to the state.

Dr. Laubach wore on his coat lapel a gold button on which were the letters "CIHU" around a globe and two hands clasped in handshake. The main object of wearing the button, he explained to me, is to cause someone to ask what it is. This gives the wearer an opportunity to explain and at the same time to get in some words for a very wholesome philosophy of life.

Not the originator of the idea – although it epitomized his lifetime of helping people all over the world – Dr. Laubach was enthusiastic in support of the movement. He said that he would like to see "cihu" take the place of our everyday "hello" that we use as a greeting. But he doubtless wanted to see more significance attached to the new greeting.

In the spirit of his proposed new greeting, Dr. Laubach spoke to the inmates of Cummins Farm (Arkansas' State Penitentiary), many of whom learned how to read and write through Laubach Literacy classes taught at the institution.

"You may think it strange of me to envy you," he said, "but you have many more years to live and I have quite possibly just a year or two. It is not too late for you to make a new beginning for your lives. Find the purpose of God for you and set yourselves to that purpose. Get all the education you can, for in knowledge is power. But as you acquire knowledge, develop integrity. All the knowledge in the world will not be worth anything if people cannot trust you."

In a further word to the prison inmates, Dr. Laubach counseled them to think of helping, rather than taking advantage of others. He gave them the new word "cihu." And he emphasized that Christ loves everyone of them, "as do many of us."

In response to the Laubach remarks, one of the prisoners expressed appreciation on behalf of the prison class and personally endorsed all that the distinguished visitor had said. Of the emphasis for integrity he said: "All of you know that we are here because we lacked integrity."

Wouldn't it be a wonderful thing if all of us could greet each other with "cihu" and really mean it?

29. Soon the Frost (Hope)

As this was written, the afternoon of October 20, our bed of crimson verbenias was still flourishing in our front yard. For weeks now I have been visiting the flowers as frequently as possible to drink in their beauty. I know they will be gone with the first killing frost.

Two weeks ago, as I was standing in front of the flowers, a black-and-orange butterfly appeared and drank thirstily from the sweet nectar of the blossoms. Considering how soon both the butterfly and the flowers must die, I felt that I was looking on Ephemera itself.

There is something sad and mystical about the feeling you

have when you know you are looking at that which is soon to die. Sometimes the doomed one is a loved one in a family – one who has a hopeless affliction or a terminal illness. The doctors have said: "Two or three months to live – six months at most." Then the relatives and friends who know about it do much as we do with the flowers about to be killed. We live from day to day, making the most of the minutes and the hours we have with the fatally-stricken loved ones.

But time after time, the one who goes next on the mysterious journey to that land "from whose bourne no one returns" is not the one with the few days or weeks to live, but one who was in good health, or was thought to have been, frequently not the aged and infirm, but the young and the strong. A slippery highway, a dozing driver, or perhaps, a failure of brakes, and then a thundering crash and a life blown out!

If we could somehow know what would be our last meeting with someone we would be tenderhearted and so thoughtful in everything. But since we cannot know and there is the real possibility that any meeting or any parting may be the last, this should temper our thoughts and our actions. After all, we have much in common with the verbenias and the butterfly. We also await the killing frost.

But through and beyond the frost there is an eternal spring:

"He who from zone to zone
Guides through the sky thy certain flight
In the long way that I must tread alone
Will guide my steps aright."

30. The Nose Knows! (Human Body)

An old German friend who used to break open his wife's hot, tasty biscuits and hold them close to his nose for a few good whiffs before beginning to devour them knew how to get the most "taste" out of his biscuits. For it is your nose, and not your taste buds, that has the most to do with all your discriminating tastes.

According to a feature in an issue of *Aetna Life Lines* entitled "Your Nose Knows," you would not be able to tell apples from onions without your nose. (Your eyes might help, for apples do not make the eyes water.)

For doubting Thomases and Thomasines, the article suggests a simple test. Simply mix some minced onion (why minced?) and apple in a dish. Then hold your nose, close your eyes and taste the mixture. You will get a sweetish flavor, it says here, but that is all.

The truth of the matter is – and I am still quoting – your tongue can discern only four flavors – sweet, sour, salty, and bitter. It is your nose that knows the difference between thousands of flavors.

The article continues:

"The odors reaching this sensitive organ (nose) can have a subtle but definite effect on mood and emotion. Certain scents may bring on nostalgia, for example, by evoking memories of a happy experience. Others may stimulate you to impulsive actions without your knowing why.

"Using this knowledge, sales psychologists can literally lead you to their wares by the nose. One couple speeded the sale of their home by keeping cakes baking in the oven when prospects came looking. Chemists are marketing an enticing "new car aroma" to spray on used cars. And researchers are ever busy developing new "sell smells" to seduce your psyche through your sniffer."

The Lord certainly had a wonderful purpose in designing the human nose. But the purpose of the high pressure salesmen does not necessarily coincide with the purpose of the Lord. So, better look twice before you "follow your nose" to market.

31. On Being Sick (Illness)

A few days of being on the ailing list has brought to mind the many differences between being sick now and forty or fifty years ago.

Most of us older folk swigged enough "fever medicine" and quinine tonic to float the proverbial battleship, as we paid for the privilege of living in mosquito country. Some of us still cannot stand chocolate flavor because of the "chocolate quinine" we swallowed. And the highly touted Coca-Cola is more than "refreshing" when your earliest recollection of it was using it to take the taste of bitter medicine out of your mouth.

Fever thermometers were nonexistent where we grew up. Mama used to determine that we had fever by laying a hand on our heads and comparing it with the feel of the heads of children who were obviously hale and hearty.

Once it was determined that you had fever, you were put to bed (or pallet) and a wet cloth laid across your head. Every few minutes, Mama, Papa, brother or sister – whichever one was the nurse in charge – would dip the brow cloth into cool water and lay it back on your head.

If the sick one's fever did not "go down" soon, a runner would be sent to town to summon the doctor. The doctor, fortified by his big pillbag that had about every kind of medicine then available, would come as soon as he could. If he already had several cases of pneumonia, malarial fever, and typhoid, he might be late arriving. But he would get there eventually.

If you got sick in winter, care was taken to keep you well wrapped. But if you came down with something in summer, whoever was tending you would fan you with a big palm leaf fan.

The value of having a family that really loved you was never more obvious than when you were sick. And one of the highlights of disability was just lying up and thinking of things you wanted or things you could ask the folks to do for you and then seeing how they would jump to please you. (This played out pretty fast once you were well on the way to convalescence. There was always the day of rude awakening when someone would tell you point-blank that if you wanted something you could get it for yourself.)

Now we do not send for the doctor, we go to him. And if the fever will not go down, they put us in air-conditioned hospital rooms equipped with telephones, radios, television, and presided over by trained nurses, and they "doctor" us with miracle drugs.

A lot more of us get well now than in the old days. But us old timers miss the coddling we had when we were "doctored" at our own firesides and nursed by our own families.

32. New Church Award (Inactivity)

A new area of church endeavor was discovered recently by Pastor James Pleitz of First Baptist Church, Pensacola, Florida.

But let Pastor Pleitz tell you about it:

"She couldn't have been any happier if she had been chosen 'Miss Kindergarten of the Year.' The precious little five-year-old girl was simply tickled pink to be selected 'The Best Rester.'

"Now I hate to reveal my ignorance, but the truth of the matter is that I had no idea what she had been selected as – or to, as the case might be.

"Her parents were kind enough to clear up the mystery. Each day a 20-minute period had been set aside for the children to rest from their kindergarten activities. During this period they were to be perfectly quiet. There was to be no talking and no moving about. Suzanne had won hands down – behold the best rester!"

You can imagine what such an experience suggested to a pastor who, as any other shepherd, always has a lot of sheep whose chief attainment is resting. But in case you are resting and too tired to use your imagination, here are the thoughts stirred in Brother Pleitz' coconut:

"It would not be an easy decision to make in most of our churches. It would be a lot easier to select the best singer, or the best teacher, or the best giver, etc. The selection would be made difficult because we have so many folk who specialize in resting.

"Some of these same people are referred to as 'balls of fire' in community activities, but when it comes to the activities of the church, you wouldn't even call them 'flickering flames.' Nay, not even 'wisps of smoke.' "

And this is about where you would expect the preacher to bring in his punch lines. And that's what Brother Pleitz did:

"The Lord said something one day about coming to him for rest. 'Come unto me all ye that labor and are heavy laden, and I will give you rest.' But read on! Jesus said, 'Take my yoke upon you, and learn of me . . . for my yoke is easy, and my burden is light.'

"Christ rests weary men with a yoke because our deepest need is to be needed and our souls are not at rest unless they are growing. And souls do not grow toward the fulness of Christ unless they 'bear one another's burdens, and so fulfill the law of Christ.' "

33. As Time Flies (Ingenuity)

A lot of life is snuffed out, for all practical purposes, by one-track-mindedness and by putting things off to supposedly more opportune times.

For example, a husband may kid himself into believing that there is nothing else he can do while mowing his wife's lawn. But, with the average cranium having the contents God has stuffed into it, a fellow can do a lot of thinking and planning in realms far removed from the drudgery (or exhilaration?) of mowing the lawn.

Are you behind with your personal correspondence? Why

not center on some letters you need to write and decide what you will say in them and how you will say it, as your body routinely follows the mower row on row across the yard? One of the hardest things about writing – and this goes for all kinds of writing – is deciding what to say and how to say it. Once you have done this, writing is pure joy.

If you are a preacher or a Sunday School teacher, you ought to get in some of your best thinking on the Scriptures and the situations you are dealing with for the sermon you are to preach or the lesson you are to teach, all while cutting the grass.

Have you been trying to make up your mind about what to do and where to go for your vacation this year? Then, as you mow, try to reach some decisions in this realm. And while you are at it, concoct some scheme for getting the plans approved by Friend Wife and the Kids.

And so on, far, far into the evening, depending on how much grass and sunlight you have. The number of worlds you can conquer is limited only by the size of your yard.

We live in an age of making and meeting appointments. Half an hour ago I learned that it would be an hour before the fellows could service my car, over at the service station. Immediately I had to adjust to the other fellow's schedule. And so you are now reading what I wrote while waiting.

Most of us have to go see doctors and dentists occasionally. And this almost always involves some waiting in the outer office. If you like to read, why not take along something worth reading? Or carry a note pad and a pencil to jot down notes on plans you can make while waiting.

Do not neglect the spiritual side of your life. Some wisely make use of "waiting" time by spending at least a part of it in meditation and silent prayer.

Time is of the essence.

34. Parable of the Cat (Ingratitude)

The couple had not wanted a cat. But the children who brought the scrawny kitten to their door on a cold night had played on their pity. So the kitten gained admission, flea colony and all, and ran crying to the family refrigerator.

The cat's new mistress went to work immediately to transform the little female into an acceptable pet. She secured for it the tastiest and most nutritious of cat foods – condensed milk, tuna, chicken, liver, etc., and any number of combinations of these. She deflead the little critter and took her to a vet for her rabies and distemper shots when she was old enough for these.

Because the cat's feet were white and resembled white boots, the mistress, with the master's hearty approval, called her "Boots." And master and mistress loved the cat and rubbed her fur – always the right way – and let her have the run of the house. They even permitted her to loll atop the television set. And they gave her a clawing pole and balls and spools and many other of the things kittens like for playthings.

Then, one day when Boots was well-nourished and her fur was in fine fettle, she suddenly decided that she did not need her master any longer. Was it not her mistress who was her constant companion and the one who fed her promptly and petted her throughout the day? Who was this character, anyhow, who stayed off somewhere else all day and then came home at night and expected her, Boots, to emote over him?

(The fact that it was her master who paid the rent and bought the groceries, including the cat groceries, seemed to make not the slightest difference in the cat's attitude. She would run away anytime the master approached.)

"What have I done to deserve this?" asked the master. "I have never stepped on the cat even accidentally and I have always been kind to her."

Suddenly it seemed God was speaking to the cat's frustrated master. "Now you see what it is like between me and my people," He was saying. "I have given you life and I have nourished you and loved you and yet many of you run from me. Some of you would not like to be caught dead in My house. You are indebted to me for all you are and all you have. Yet, you are afraid of me and you despise me."

And that's the parable of the ungrateful cat.

35. "The Hand That Feeds" (Ingratitude)

The beggar's appearance belied her plea of destitution. For her frock of predominate gold blending with black and grey was neat and well tailored and it could not hide the fact that the wearer was pleasingly plump.

But what can you do but find food, for one who comes to your door for a handout?

So I quickly found something. I gave her what was closest at hand – papershell pecans. And she ate as one famished.

She had consumed eight or ten of the huge nuts when, all at once, it happened.

I was holding out to her another pecan when she suddenly passed up the nut to grab my hand and sink her sharp teeth into my thumb. Only by painful and physical force was I able to break her cannibalistic hold. As she let go and blood covered my aching thumb, she gave me a startled, hurt look, as if I had been the unfriendly and cruel one, and away she ran.

I had to admit that while I was not, really, squirrel-headed, as critics sometimes allege, I actually now was squirrel-bitten. And that by a female of the fox squirrel species who had stuffed herself on my pecans!

"Biting the hand that feeds you" is a strong and familiar figure of speech. I do not know who first used the expression. According to Bartlett's *Familiar Quotations,* it was used by the noted British statesman Edmund Burke (1729-97) in an address titled "Thoughts and Details on Security." Said Mr.

Burke: "And having looked to government for bread, on the very first scarcity they will turn and bite the hand that fed them."

How do you bite the hand that feeds you?

There must be at least a million ways. For any time you show hostility or ingratitude to one to whom you are indebted, you bite the hand that feeds you.

The son or daughter who in any way despises or brings dishonor upon parents whose sacrifices brought that one into the world and cared tenderly for him or her through many a helpless year is biting the hand that feeds.

The husband or wife who rebuffs a companion's love with any degree of cruelty or unfaithfulness is biting the hand that feeds.

The wayward one for whom Chirst died, who insists on going his own way and will not live for the One who died for him, is biting the hand that feeds him.

But as painful as it is to have your hand bitten by one you are feeding, is it not much better to be the feeder than the biter?

36. Pew, Pew, Pew (Involvement)

On one of Dr. Frank C. Laubach's visits to Arkansas, I went with the noted "Apostle to the Illiterates" to introduce him as he was to speak to a college student assembly.

As the students came into the auditorium, they contended with each other for the very back seats. When all were seated, there were many rows of empty seats immediately in front of the speaker's platform.

Dr. Laubach reacted to the situation in a most unexpected way. When I had completed a rather glowing introduction, the noted missionary stood briefly before the microphone of the public-address system and announced in obvious disgust: "I am going to sit down and give you time to move to the front. When you have moved, I'll speak." And he sat down!

There was a moment's hesitation and then the whole student body moved forward.

Beaming appreciation, Dr. Laubach then began his address with warm words of gratitude that went far toward wiping out any resentment he had stirred. Soon the students were "eating out of his hand."

"You can't do much good as a speaker if your audience is not with you and helping you," said Dr. Laubach to me after the chapel service and as we were on our way to another engagement.

One thing I noticed was that Dr. Laubach would never begin to speak on any occasion without first saying to the group he was to address: "I need your help. Will each of you pray for me while I speak?"

Dr. Laubach was a great man of prayer. He knew there are incalculable blessings that come through prayer. But he confessed to me that there are some very desirable side benefits from leading a congregation to pray for the speaker.

"People cannot pray for the speaker and be hostile to him all at the same time," he said. "And people cannot be praying for the speaker and be talking among themselves. Neither can they sleep while they pray!"

Just a few in a congregation who are openly hostile to the speaker can greatly hurt the spirit of the service. There are many ways to show opposition. Of course, sitting far to the rear when there are seats up front is one way. Other ways, often indulged in by those seated fartherest out, include yawning every little while, looking at one's watch, dozing, talking to someone, reading a book, writing, doodling, sitting directly behind a post or somebody else so that the speaker cannot see your face.

One of the hardest assignments is that of preaching to a congregation that does not want to feel any involvement along with the preacher.

37. Joy versus Pleasure (Joy)

Something in a recent Sunday School lesson pointed up the great difference between pleasure and joy.

You can have either one without the other. But if you must choose between the two, joy is much more substantial than pleasure.

The thing that brought the superiority of joy over pleasure to mind was this from Paul's letter to the Romans:

"For if while we were enemies we were reconciled to God by the death of His Son, much more, now that we are reconciled, shall we be saved by his life. Not only so, but we also rejoice in God through our Lord Jesus Christ, through whom we have now received our reconciliation" (Rom. 5:10-11, RSV).

The pleasures of sin are not worthy to be compared with the joys of salvation.

The surest and most universal characteristic of one whose sins have been forgiven – for one who has been reconciled to God – is joy. So the professing Christian who goes around with a long face, who has no sense of humor, and who devotes his time and energies to serving as a spiritual policeman, trying to make everybody else conform to his own pattern of living, has missed the boat. He may be as sincere as Paul was as a Pharisee persecuting Christians, but he is also just about as far away from outwardly manifesting Christianity.

It is only when pleasure is equated with godly living that it can be taken as being synonymous with the joy of which Paul speaks. Paul uses the word this way in 2 Corinthians 12:10: "For the sake of Christ, then, I am content with [take pleasure in] weakness, insults, hardships, persecutions, and calamities; for when I am weak then I am strong."

Paul is himself the best example of what I am talking about. Take a look at just one of many incidents in his life, the beating and jailing he and Silas experienced at Phillipi. Certainly there was no pleasure here, as we usually think of the word. But the ordeal could not take away the joy of these great heroes of the Christian faith. So, at midnight, they sang joyful hymns.

Even in sorrow, heart-break, affliction, and death, the flame of joy never goes out in the heart of the Christian. So:

"May the God of hope fill you with a joy and peace in believing, so that by the power of the Holy Spirit you may abound in hope" (Rom. 15:13, RSV).

38. Why You Are You (Kinship)

Many years ago I visited an aging uncle who lived in a distant state. I had not seen him for many years and was amazed at what I learned about myself on that visit. He and I differed greatly as far as age, education, viewpoints, and habits were concerned. But the amazing thing to me was how much we were alike.

If you want to understand better what you are like, take a good look at your family. Pay particular attention to the older members whom you are privileged to know personally. Thus you may gain a pretty good idea not only as to what you are likely to look like a few years hence, but what you are like now and what you will get to be like.

From studying your family you can understand better why you are tall or short, thin or fat, fair or dark, small-boned or big-boned; why your eyes are blue, brown, green, or hazel; why your ears, your nose, your feet, your hands are huge, small or in-between. You may also get some tip as to why you are quick-tempered and energetic or good-humored and easy-going. You certainly can get a pretty good idea as to your life expectancy by taking note of how long your parents, grandparents, great-grandparents, and your uncles and aunts lived.

All of this and much more you can learn about yourself just by studying your family. Where we live, the people we are thrown with or who are thrown with us, the books we read, the things we do for a living, what we enjoy as pastime, our religious faith or lack of faith – all of these help to shape us and make us what we are and what we are becoming.

That where we have lived leaves its mark upon us is reflected by the fact that you can usually spot quickly someone who grew up in the deep South, or out West, or up East.

But the most vital environmental effect comes from association with people. Every one of us has an effect upon the opinions, the prejudices, and the conduct of others. And each of us is shaped to some extent – and for better or for worse – by every one he meets.

This highlights the importance of our getting to know the greatest of all persons – Jesus Christ. Here is one whose influence upon us cuts across heredity and environment to take us as we are and make us what we ought to be.

More than anything else, you and I are what we are because of whether or not we are associated with Christ.

39. A Comma Missing (Little Things)

Just how important is punctuation?

It may make all the difference in the world, says Roy Lyon, promoter for lay training, Venezuela.

"They left out a comma in the 1960 Revision of the Spanish Version of the Bible," he writes, "and changed the whole direction of my ministry."

The passage in question is Ephesians 4:11-13, quoted here with the missing comma in parentheses:

"And his gifts were that some should be apostles, some prophets, some evangelists, some pastors and teachers, for the equipment of the saints (,) for the work of the ministry, for the building up of the body of Christ, until we all attain to the unity of the faith and of the knowledge of the Son of God, to mature manhood, to the full measure of the stature of the fulness of Christ."

As he looked into the situation, Missionary Lyon discovered that the comma in question had previously been added to the text by commentators but that there is no such comma in the ancient manuscripts.

What difference did the absence of this one little comma make? Says Lyon: "If Christians can get the idea of what a great difference the absence of that little comma makes, it will be like opening the gate and channeling the mighty waters behind the dam through a huge dynamo. Power can be released that has been stagnant for ages."

The difference this comma makes is the difference between an exclusive ministry of the clergy and a ministry for laymen "in a secular world where the 'church' and the 'clergy' have been recently excluded," says Lyon. He quotes a footnote from *The Oxford Annotated Bible*: "It is better to omit the comma after 'saints'; all Christians are to be equipped for the work of actual spiritual service."

Concludes Missionary Lyon: "Consciously or unconsciously, the scholars who put that comma in the text were clergymen who felt that the ministry belonged to them, and not to the layman. For them, the clergy was the Church."

What a difference the absence of one comma does make!

40. Truth in Advertising (Lucidity)

Truth may or may not be stranger than fiction. Perhaps we would need to ask, What truth is stranger than what fiction? But sometimes the advertisements are more interesting reading than the rest of a publication.

For a long time I have been amused by the things Avis (the car rental service) puts in their ads. This is the only firm I know of that spends money to brag about being *second* in its field. Avis says a business that is second and not first really has to be sure that its service is all the customer could hope for. It must pay to be humble!

Something from a recent ad by Hertz, contemporary of Avis, made me prick up my ears: "It's the underdog that's keeping the top dog on top."

Still on the subject of interesting advertising, I am going to predict that a little college over in New York State will reap a profitable harvest of contributions and/or inquiries from donors and prospective donors as the result of a full-page ad in one of the national news magazines.

Declared little Franconia College, of Franconia, New York, in the opening paragraph:

"We need money. Not to grow in size, but in quality. Not so much to build buildings as to develop men and women who can keep on growing after graduation to meet the needs of a changing society."

And I liked the way the ad writers slipped up on their readers with what the college is really doing. That is always a vital part of any fund-raising pitch. But it is not always couched in such human-interest, down-to-earth language as that in the Franconia ad:

"If you choose to contribute to Franconia you may find your funds invested in a program which will send a student to Alaska to study life in an Eskimo village, to the lower East Side of New York to examine problems, to take English history at our Franconia-in-Oxford branch, or even to another college. Franconia students have already done all these and more – the world is becoming our laboratory for learning."

What a great encouragement these ads bring us. If the underdog has a part in keeping the top dog on top, then the underdog is not a complete failure. And if the world is a laboratory for learning, even the remotest one of us is always in the laboratory!

41. On Riding Double (Marriage)

A young couple "riding double" on a motorcycle – a lad and a lass – turned abruptly in front of my car as I was driving home from work the other day. Fortunately, there was room for the unexpected maneuvering and no crash occurred.

The young lady, riding back of the driver, could not have been in on the quick decision to turn. But she went right along with the pilot and his decision. She neither moved to dismount nor to take over the control. There had evidently been a definite and far-reaching commitment on her part when she had mounted the 'cycle.

Whether she had said it in so many words, she had at least said in her action: "I will go with you. I will trust you to drive safely and sanely. Whatever you decide as to the operation of the vehicle, I am with you for the duration of our spin together. I trust you completely."

How different this is from the way many a couple runs its marital affairs. So much of the time there is no agreement as to which of the two is at the "controls." All too frequently, husband and wife spend their energy – and spin their wheels – over who is the head of the family.

Running a home is a lot like riding double on a motorcycle. There is need for both parties to the deal to realize that "we are in this together." And just as two could not travel very far by motorcycle if they could never agree on who was to be in the driver's seat, husband and wife will be hopelessly frustrated unless a similar decision is reached in the family situation.

In this column you would expect to find the male viewpoint. All I have to say is that of all the couples I have seen riding double on motorcycles, I have not yet seen a woman in the driver's seat with a man riding back of her. But I have known many a sad family situation in which the wife "wore the pants."

Someone has said: "The man, at the head of the house,

can mar the pleasure of the household, but he cannot make it. That must rest with the woman, and it is her greatest privilege."

Bill Tillett has said: "God help the man who won't marry until he finds a perfect woman, and God help him still more if he finds her."

42. Smoking Chimneys (Mistakes)

Sometime ago I went with some friends to see their newly remodelled, country home. The work was almost finished, but the family had not yet moved in.

The appealing feature of the re-made home, now to have modern facilities, was a well-equipped and modern kitchen and a most attractive den opening off of it.

The real eye-catcher was a beautiful, wide fireplace at the end of the den and opposite the kitchen. It was obvious that the family had not skimped on building this chimney. They had secured nothing but the best building stone and had made the fireplace big enough to burn sizeable logs. The chimney was topped off with a beautifully appointed mantle.

A few weeks later I was back for a visit with these friends, now set up in the new home. But I was somewhat shocked on entering the kitchen-den to discover the room was being heated by a large gas stove which had been set up on the hearth of the fireplace. I had hoped to sit before a roaring, open fire, such as many of us grew around – perhaps burning me on one side and freezing me on the other – remember?

They were not long in telling me what had happened. The day they moved in, they built a fire in the new fireplace and soon had to flee for fresh air. Instead of drawing the smoke up and out the top, the pretty, new chimney puffed it out into the new room.

"But what of the man who built the chimney?" I asked. "Have you told him, and has he been over to see about it?"

"You can be sure he knows," they replied. The chimney builder had come over and stood before the fire and said, "It's not supposed to do that!" But it kept on puffing the smoke out into the room as long as there was any fire left.

"What are you going to do about it?" I asked.

"Not but one thing we can do," replied the husband, "and that's tear it down and build another. This time we'll be sure it is built right."

Building mistakes are not always confined to rock chimneys. Sometimes it is lives that are involved. But even then, with God's help, we can start over and build again.

43. A Little Friend (Nature)

Aren't you glad the Lord made the mockingbird? For several mornings in a row now one of these delightful entertainers has made our alarm clock excess equipment as it has favored us with a pre-dawn serenade from a perch just outside our bedroom window. The great variety of sounds this beloved mimic can blend into song is amazing. For it does not restrict itself to the sounds of fellow birds, but occasionally will pick up something from man's technological achievements. And no two mockers have identical repertoires. These little creatures, even as you and I, are largely shaped by their environments.

There used to be a practice of people robbing nests of fledgling mockingbirds to provide captive songsters. And, it is reported, being prisoners for life in the cramped quarters of bird cages did not dampen the ardor of the singers. Fortunately, this predatory barbarity has long since been outlawed by legislatures across the land. Bird lovers can lobby, too, you know!

The mockingbird is undoubtedly one of the most courageous of all of God's creatures. Let it get the impression that its nest or its little ones are being molested and it will mount a dive-bombing attack that can make life miserable for whatever happens to be the target.

Many a time have I seen the mockingbird venting its spleen in effective battle against the much larger jays and hawks. And just the other day I saw one dive-bombing the Ellis McCorkle tomcat. The cat, no doubt wisened by previous attacks, pursued the technique of just ignoring the bird and remaining completely immoble as it sunbathed on the patio. That must have taken some real will power, for the flogging continued for several minutes. And each time the enraged bird dived, it let out a savage screech that would have been worthy of the most uninhibited Comanche on the warpath.

Paraphrasing what the late Ardis Tyson said about his hound, there are days when you'd feel that you did not have a friend in the world if it were not for the mockingbird outside your window.

44. Our Jay's Solo (Nature)

Our family feels a little less of the weight of the world on its shoulders now – the two baby jaybirds have successfully soloed from their nest in the top of one of our front-yard pines and are well on the way to becoming orientated to this big world.

The little tykes seemed to have their heads together as to when they would leave their mother's nest. Just about suppertime Friday night, my wife heard a rather jolting contact with the side of our house and discovered one of the birds was on the ground. A few minutes later, and in about the same flight pattern, the other one was down – also colliding with the side of the house. But neither seemed to be injured.

The jay parents were keeping an eye on the project and talking what sounded like jaybird baby talk. They seemed to understand that my wife and I were there to help and not to harm their little ones. Even when I picked the little ones up, one at a time, to carry them to the safer environs of our fenced-in back yard, and with the babies crying bloody murder, the parent birds still did not get excited.

As we saw the helplessness of the birds not yet able to fly and thought of the neighborhood cats and other natural enemies of birds, our hearts went out to them. We thought of the Lord's assurance that not even one sparrow "shall fall on the ground without your Father" (Matt. 10:29b); but what about *two jays?* Well, you have to be more than a strict literalist to be assured of the presence of the Heavenly Father in this situation, for jays are not specifically mentioned by name in the Bible. But they are included in many places in general terms.

Who but God provided for these little jays to have the protecting care of their parents on their lonely flight into the big, wide world?

Let us not forget the lesson the Lord was trying to teach us when he spoke of the falling sparrow:

"But the very hairs of your head are all numbered. Fear ye not therefore, ye are more value than many sparrows. Whosoever therefore shall confess me before men, him will I confess also before my Father, which is in heaven" (Matt. 10:30-32).

The next morning the baby jays were still there, trying their wings on the back of our yard. The parents were still hovering near. And so, I felt, also was God.

45. Red-feathered Friends (Nature)

Among wild neighbors I like best is the redbird.

The redbird has many aliases: "cardinal grosbeak," "crested redbird," and "Virginia nightingale," to mention a few. But as far as I am concerned, a redbird is a redbird. They all look and sound pretty much alike.

It was as a boy cane-pole fishing for "perch" (bluegills or

bream, to many of you) that I first fell for redbirds. It seemed to me that fishing was best on those spring and summer days when the redbirds were perching in nearby trees and doing their delightful whistling routines. Even when you are fishing solitare, you never feel lonesome with a friendly redbird trilling in your vicinity.

Unlike many others of our bird friends, redbirds do not fly away to escape our mid-American winters. They are with us through all four seasons. This is made possible by the fact that the redbird is not too particular about his meals. If the cold weather destroys the insects he likes to eat, he can get along nicely, thank you, on weed seeds and other things still available even in the dead of winter.

The redbird, as Neltje Blanchan points out in *Birds Every Child Should Know,* is "a little smaller than a robin (not half so graceful)." The male of the species is "red all over, except a small black area around his red bill," and "he wears his head-feathers crested like the blue jay and the titmouse."

When my wife and I were having a hard time keeping blackbirds and sparrows from gorging down the "hen scratch" from the feed boxes in our backyard, to the exclusion of our redbird friends, some fellow birdlovers advised us that redbirds like to eat early and late. Have no feed out, they said, except early and late, and then just enough for one feeding.

This works for the neighbors, and I am sure it would work for us. But we cannot forego the longing to have feed out for all comers.

Every time I see a redbird I thank the Lord for giving us this colorful and cheery outdoor friend.

46. Above Circumstances (New Year)

"Do not pray for easy lives. Pray to be stronger men! Do not pray for tasks equal to your powers. Pray for powers equal to your tasks."

This counsel from Phillips Brooks (1835-1893) is timely for all of us as we begin the new year.

In our day the timid soul may keep himself insulated from life by staying soused in liquor or tranquilizers. But such ones do not really live, they just exist and it is a sorry existence.

There is a story of two brothers who were caught stealing sheep. The penalty assessed by a jury of their neighbors was that such should have branded in his forehead the letters "S" and "T," for "sheep thief."

One of the brothers, unable to live with the stigma, went out to a far country, where he wandered aimlessly and finally died of bitterness. The other brother decided that he would stay at home and live such a life that his neighbors would come to respect him. "I cannot run away from the fact that I once stole some sheep," he said.

As the years went by, he built a reputation for integrity. One day, when he was an old man, a stranger saw him with "S.T." on his forehead and asked a neighbor of the man about it.

"It happened a long time ago," said the neighbor. "I do not remember the particulars, but I think it stands for 'Saint.'"

The ones who make the most of this new year will not be the ones who do not have anything happen to them. Rather, they will be the ones who are able to rise above circumstances which, on the face of them, may appear hard and hopeless.

Those who have the best prospects for living abundantly and victoriously this year are those who have not only their own resources but the resource of God on which to draw:

"I waited patiently for the Lord and he inclined unto me, and heard my cry.

"He brought me up also out of an horrible pit, out of the miry clay, and set my feet upon a rock, and established my goings.

"And he hath put a new song in my mouth, even praise unto our God. . . ." (Ps. 40:1-3).

It is easy to walk in a new way when you walk with your hand in the hand of God.

47. Come in, New Year (New Year)

In these days of living better or worse "electrically," our homes come equipped with outside buttons for the operation of inside doorbells.

This modern counterpart of the colorful "latchstring" which in more primitive times was "always hanging on the outside" to friends, is there for any and all to press who pass our way. But when you get down to the brass tacks of the situation, the button is primarily for our friends and acquaintances. For we are always a little reluctant to open the door and invite into our homes "perfect strangers." We want to know of the doorbell ringer, "Who are you and what do you want?" though we may find a more polite and less direct way of putting it.

Sometimes we find it necessary, for one reason or another, to admit a stranger. Such was the case just this week as we came to the end of the old year and found a brand new year standing at our door.

As we reflect on what the old year turned out to be, some of us might be inclined to close our doors in the face of the new year and pretend we are not at home. But here is one stranger who cannot be kept out, whether we like it or not. Yet, despite the fact that this newcomer is the very epitome of the unknown and the unknowable, he is something of a "star boarder" in that he will be around every day for a full twelve months, fifty-two weeks. And although he is to be here for a comparatively short time, some of us will depart ahead of him.

Since there is nothing else we can do, anyway, we may as well be polite and say, "Come in, new year, and make yourself at home. We'll take you as you come, a day at a time, and with the Lord's help, we will do the best we can for you."

And we can thank our God that in His kindness of not revealing the future to us in advance, He lets us know that He holds both us and the future.

48. "Yes-s-s you are!" (Parenthood)

While walking down a hospital corridor the other day I got a glimpse of a young mother having one of her first visits – if not the very first – with her new baby. And I was reminded again of what a wonderful thing God has ordained in the parent-child bond.

My attention was attracted to the scene by the endearing words of the mother, directed to her little one: "Yes-s-s, you are! Yes-s-s, you are! "– with strong emphasis on the "yes."

I do not know what had gone before, but I suppose the mother had already said something like, "You are the sweetest little fellow in all the world!"

As the mother talked, lying on a slightly elevated bed, she held her offspring on an arm, stretching him (or her) full length before her. And it was easy to see that the new arrival was really basking in the mother's love. As the little one listened – charmed, it appeared, at his mother's voice – his arms and legs gyrated.

A baby is a lot like any other pet – only it takes longer to housebreak. But a baby is, of course, much, much more than a mere pet. He is a human being endowed by his Creator with almost unlimited potential for change and development. And the baby is not long in showing that he not only has his mother's good points, but also his father's bad points.

It takes a baby many months to communicate in meaningful words, phrases, and sentences. But he is a good communicator from the beginning. For he learns from the start that one or more members of the household will come running just about anytime of the day or night that he lets out a howl. So, whether he longs for a new diaper or for his next feeding, or is just lonesome for a little cuddling, he starts screaming.

But adding to the family circle a newcomer who is bald, toothless, talkless and walkless – one who can neither feed himself nor dress himself, and one who soaks up loving attention as a sponge – really throws the old family routine into a tailspin.

Whether the baby is the only child in the family or just one of a series, his coming adds tremendously to the responsibilities of the fellow who is the only husband and the lady who is the only wife. And nothing is more essential to the happiness of the family and the healthy and normal unfolding of the little one (or ones) than having enough love to go around. For everybody has an inalienable right to feel that he is always a V.I.P. in his own family.

"Yes-s-s, you are!"

49. What's Your P.E.Q.? (People)

Do people bother you?

Is it your honest conviction that there are too many other rats in the race?

Have you found that there are too many people trying to get on or off the freeway at the times you want to get on or off the freeway?

Do too many people insist on buying their groceries at the time you want to buy yours?

If you are of the fair sex, do too many women flash new hats, frocks, pumps, and purses just like the ones you are flashing?

Is your foursome being jostled on the local green?

Do too many Isaac Waltons beat you to your favorite spots at Lake Conway or Lake Maumelle, or Bull Shoals?

Do you sometimes share the sentiments of the little girl who said to her playmate in a not-so-large sand box: "If one of us would get out of the box, I'd have more room"?

Are you a purple people hater? What is your P.E.Q. – People Endurance Quotient?

Let me remind you that the P.E.Q. of some of the first disciples of our Lord was not all that might have been desired.

There was at least one time when some of them wanted to call down napalm from heaven upon people who had not been as respectful to them as they (the disciples) felt they should have been. (See Luke 9:54.)

And some of the religious leaders of the day were so angered at the good life of Jesus that they tried to destroy him. (The only thing that kept them from succeeding was the power of the Resurrection.)

The Lord himself had no P.E.Q. at all. For when you love someone, you don't endure him, you die for him. And that's what the Lord did for every member of the mob that finally lynched him – and for every last one of us.

When our Lord was caught in a crowd, his heart went out to the people – "But when he saw the multitudes, he was moved with compassion on them . . ." (Matt. 9:36).

If we are to be true disciples of the Lord, we must be able with his help to do more than endure people – we must love them.

And if you think that is a tough assignment, think of what it is like for those who are obligated to love you and me!

50. What Time Is It? (Perspective)

"It is later than you think" is something heard so often that we do not pay much attention to it – unless something in our own personal experience drives it home to us.

At our house, we depend more on the early morning sun to get us out of bed than the blast of an alarm clock. But one morning recently the Lord left the shades of the morning pulled down and we overslept. When I finally got up, thinking the time was about 6:15, I was surprised to learn that, instead, it was 7:45! It really was later than I thought!

In his letter to the Christians in Rome, Paul had his own way of saying to them, "It is later than you think":

"The night is far spent, the day is at hand: let us therefore cast off the works of darkness, and let us put on the armor of light" (Rom. 13:12).

As so often is the case, the Scriptures here start with something familiar to people in their everyday lives and go on to make a spiritual application. The first and obvious thing Paul says is that nighttime, the time for repose, when the work of the daytime could not be done, was past and a new day was well underway. So, it was time to get out of bed and get dressed and get to work.

But there is a higher meaning. For "night," as used in the Bible, not only denotes night in the usual sense, but ignorance and crime and moral and spiritual darkness. Here, as suggested by Albert Barnes in his *Notes on the New Testament*, "it seems to denote our present imperfect and obscure condition in this world, as contrasted with the pure light of heaven."

Some may see in this a frightful warning that our lives are swiftly passing and that they will soon be over, here on earth. Certainly that is implied. But there is also the brighter side: "The day is at hand."

When the Christian comes to the end of his days here, he is only at the beginning of the endless days of living in the presence of God.

"The night is far spent, the day is at hand" is a good thought to begin each new day. For, as our Lord himself admonished:

"I must work the works of him that sent me, while it is day: the night cometh, when no man can work."

51. When You Lose Your Vote (Politics)

There is something stimulating and, frequently, frustrating in the atmosphere of an election in which there are many "hot" issues and hard-fought races. Sometimes tempers flare and friendships are strained because of differing viewpoints and loyalties.

One great temptation is to give a very low intellectual rating to one who took the other side of the question from you or even to question or impugn the other fellow's motives. This is especially the case with an issue viewed by many as being a moral issue. But if we are going to be democratic and Christian, we need to give as much thought to having an open mind as to having an open mouth.

Much of the differences on political matters, as on other things, comes from having "more heat than light" on the subjects or persons involved. So we must be concerned not only with getting out the vote, but with doing whatever we can to be intelligent and conscientious and to encourage others to be likewise.

Just after an election is a good time, as just before an election, to look at the place of religion in politics.

Many would agree that the Christian religion is a religion that permeates – or ought to permeate – every aspect and area of our lives. This would certainly include political affairs. And, this being true, we Christians should take our citizenship responsibilities seriously.

To be good citizens means not only to try to keep abreast of what is taking place, but actually to become personally and positively involved in civic, community, and state affairs, as well as in church affairs. Life would be a lot simpler if we could just be "good church members" without becoming otherwise involved. But we are in no better position to build spiritual tabernacles on the mountaintops and dwell there permanently than were Peter, James, and John at the transfiguration of our Lord.

When you lose your vote on what you regarded as an issue

or a personality of great import, you can take some comfort in the reflection that many other voters lost too.

Regardless of what happened in the latest election, as Christians we can resolve all over again to try with the Lord's help to be better Christians and better citizens from now on. And here there should be no conflict of interest.

52. Effectual Prayer (Prayer)

An aged mother could not resist the temptation of trying to be independent beyond her physical ability. Although confined to her bed, she tried one day, in the absence of her daughter from the room, to get up and walk across the room. But she was too weak to stand.

Hearing her mother fall, the daughter ran to her and helped her back onto the bed. When the mother was recovered enough to speak, she said to her daughter, "I will never try to walk again without first calling you."

A few weeks later the mother died. But what she had said continues to be fresh in the daughter's memory and in her spiritual experience. For, as she told us recently in a prayer meeting, "My mother's promise inspired me to make a promise of my own. I have promised the Lord never to try to walk without first calling Him."

Perhaps one of the saddest indictments of most of us is that we claim the Lord's help so infrequently.

"Confess your faults one to another, and pray for one another, that ye may be healed," James urged. And he reminded: "The effectual fervent prayer of a righteous man availeth much" (James 5:16).

This is no bright promise for the man who is living an ungodly life, or who, otherwise righteous, does not pray. The "availeth much" here draws a sharp contrast between our weakness and God's strength, between our bankrupcty and God's unlimited resources.

Ask, seek, knock, said Jesus:

"Ask, and it shall be given you; seek, and ye shall find; knock, and it shall be opened unto you: For every one that asketh receiveth; and he that seeketh findeth; and to him that knocketh it shall be opened" (Matt. 7:7-8).

Says James, the Lord's brother in the flesh as well as in the spirit:

"Ye lust, and have not: ye kill, and desire to have, and cannot obtain: ye fight and war, yet ye have not, because ye ask not. Ye ask, and receive not, because ye ask amiss, that ye may consume it upon your lusts" (James 4:2-3).

A part of the righteousness of the man whose prayers are effectual is the right motivation. He wants nothing except it be something for the furtherance of his Christian ministry in the world.

53. Blind Man's Buff (Prejudice)

"A blind man drives this truck."

This was the reassuring (?) line printed neatly across the rear doors of a delivery truck just ahead of me in the downtown Little Rock traffic one afternoon.

My first reaction was, "Oh, yeah!" as I took note of the fact that the driver was stopping for red lights and starting again on green.

One thing was obvious, the driver was not blind physically, although a blind person with the required fee might conceivably secure a driver's license.

I suppose this sign was somebody's idea of something funny. Or it may be that the admonition was really, "Be just as careful not to run over me or let me run over you as you would be if you knew for a fact that I was actually blind." That would make sense!

At this stage I took off my reporter's cap and donned my philosopher's beret. Physical blindness is just one way for one to be blind, I mused, chin in hand. As great a handicap as physical blindness is, it may well be that this lacks a lot of being as tragic as, say, intellectual, spiritual, or moral blindness – or a combination of all of these!

I recalled the request of a friend who came to me sometime ago and asked to borrow from me all the materials I had *against* a certain national organization. At first I had thought he was teasing. But he was not. He had tried the organization on the basis of an unfair and unfavorable propaganda crusade against it, had found it guilty, and refused to be swayed by whatever the facts might be. He was set blindly to prepare a paper *against* the organization.

Most of us are blind in many ways. It is easy for us to be blind to the needs of others as we center on self. "Lord, bless me and my wife, our son John and his wife, us four and no more!"

We are blinded by our prejudices. We really do not like the handicapped – handicapped educationally, economically, socially. (A certain church leader vetoed a committee's plans to invite a noted Christian speaker, because the man has a deformed face! He contended that the speaker's physical ugliness might hurt the program!)

Space fails me. But maybe all of us should wear above our car's taillights:

"A blind man (or woman) drives this vehicle"!

54. Who, Me? (Prejudice)

Prejudice is something that afflicts somebody else – not me. So I can sit back and enjoy a discussion by the "Panel of American Women" on man's inhumanity to man.

When panel member Mrs. Green – who is not green, but chocolate – got to telling about mean things some white people in her neighborhood had done to her family because of their race, I could turn my deplorer on full blast. I have never mistreated any Negro neighbors – maybe some of my white neighbors, but never any Negro neighbors. But, of course, I live in an all-white neighborhood.

Catholic Mrs. Beck upset me a little when she said that people of her faith do not all think alike and that they can do some thinking, even about matters of religion, without first being in touch with the Pope, or even a priest. For example, she said that while some Catholics regard the practice of abstaining from the eating of meats on Fridays as being equally important spiritually with loving one's neighbor, that some of them do not see that it is too important, really, what one eats or when he eats it.

Mrs. Murphy, the Presbyterian lady who served as moderator of the panel, got pretty personal, I thought, when she said: "Any fence we build to keep others out also stands as a fence to keep us in." You don't suppose she was hinting that there are *white* ghettoes of our own making, do you?

Another Presbyterian member of the panel, Mrs. Ledbetter, who said that she has no trouble not being prejudiced against races, confessed that she does have a continuing battle dealing fairly and open-mindedly with people who do not see things the way she does.

The Jewish member of the panel, Mrs. Phillips, said that she saw no reason why people cannot be friendly with one another and good neighbors, even when they differ racially, culturally, in religion, and in other ways.

As I said, I am not prejudiced myself. But I sure feel sorry for people who are not white, Southern Baptist Democrats.

55. God Is My Pilot (Providence)

A flying missionary has sent me the following excerpts from a pilot's adaption of Psalm 23:

The Lord is my pilot, I shall not falter.
He sustaineth me as I span the heavens;
He leadeth me, steady, o'er the skyways . . .
Yea, though I fly through treacherous storms and darkness
I shall fear no evil, for He is with Me . . .
Surely, His goodness and mercy

Shall accompany me each moment in the air
And I shall dwell in His matchless heavens forever.

As I have reflected on the flying I have done as a preacher-editor, two verses from another Psalm – the 139th – have come to have special meaning:

"If I take the wings of the morning, and dwell in the uttermost parts of the sea;

"Even there shall thy hand lead me, and thy right hand shall hold me" (vv. 9 and 10).

Man has always been able to take inspiring flights of the imagination, as did David three thousand years ago in these marvelous verses on the loving presence and providence of God in his life.

Today, when scientists have made it possible for us literally to "take the wings of the morning, and dwell in the uttermost parts of the sea," is it not tragic if we have less of a sense of God's presence, in jet transports, than David had with his shepherd's crook on the remote hillsides of Palestine?

When the multitudes who had been attracted to Jesus for bread lost interest as he tried to talk to them about "the bread of life" and many of them "walked no more with him," Jesus turned to his apostles and asked: "Will you also go away?" Peter was wise above measure in his response to this piercing probe. He did not say, "*Where* can we go?" There were many, many *places* to which they could have gone – including favorite fishing spots in the Sea of Galilee. But Peter asked: "To *whom* shall we go?"

There are indeed many places to which we can go today, and we can get to them in record time. But the great need of our lives is not to be geographically oriented or economically, socially, or politically oriented. Rather, our one need above all other needs is to be spiritually oriented, to have the right relationship, personally, with God, the Great and All-sufficient, Loving Person. And "no man cometh to the Father" but by Jesus the Christ.

56. "I Am with You" (Providence)

If adversity were as bad for us as many are inclined to feel that it is, surely God would not allow it to happen to his faithful ones. Some of the greatest Christians are those who live their lives, and that victoriously, in spite of tremendous and multitudinous adversities.

Adoniram and Ann Hasseltine Judson, the first Baptist foreign missionaries from the United States, are spectacular examples.

All of their friends had warned the Judsons not to go to Burma. Yet, when forced to leave India, they boarded the only available ship, the Burma-bound *Georgiana.* Aboard this old, creaking, smelly Portuguese ship Mrs. Judson was to give birth to her first child, a son, with no one to attend her but her husband. And from this desolate craft she was to see the little form of the child, still-born, consigned to the waters of the Indian Ocean.

The first night the Judsons were in Burma, an English businessman there urged Judson: "My dear sir, let an older man advise you – a man who knows his Burma. I know what I am talking about when I say to you, go back to America! Go back tonight. There's nothing here but heartache. These people have a fine, strong religion [Buddhism] of their own. They'll resent you. And while they're the kindest, pleasantest people in the world they're also the most passionate and cruel. Go back while you're still a youth full of the fire of your faith!"

But the young man who had resolved "to obey Jesus at all costs" replied: "Sir, my wife and I have come to stay."

The three-room hovel which the Judsons were invited by an English missionary couple to share was outside the Rangoon city wall, by order of the Viceroy. It was on the edge of the dump for the city's refuse, and, as O.K. and Marjorie Moore Armstrong, report in their book *The Indomitable Baptists,* "the stench was heavy and constant."

What was even more upsetting to the young missionaries

was the fact that nearby was an open field used as the place for executing criminals. (And a "criminal" might be anyone who even unwittingly offended the Viceroy or one of his numerous officials.)

Report the Armstrongs: "The cries of victims, ignored by the passersby, became almost unendurable to the sensitive Americans: the screams of men and women being beaten to death with clubs, the muffled pleas of those being buried alive, the shrieks of those disembowled and left in the blazing sun to be attacked by vultures while still alive."

The Lord does not promise those who would follow him that the way will be easy. But he does promise that the way will not be lonely – "I am with you always . . ." (Matt. 28:20).

57. Good for What? (Purpose)

An editorial in *The Montgomery Advertiser* referred to a man on the West Coast who built a marvelous machine in his garage.

Using surplus parts, he produced a machine that contained just about every mechanical and electrical device known to modern technology. On the builder's command, the huge machine, with its thousands of parts – gears, motors, relays, actuators, servo-mechanism, and so forth – would begin their complex operations.

From a control panel in the middle of the machine, the operator watched with satisfaction as lights blinked on and off to indicate all was going well, or, occasionally, that some section was in trouble.

Technicians rated the machine a marvel. There was just one sad note. The machine was designed and built to do nothing! It was "magnum opus of a gadgeter who was carried away with the wonders of the machine age." He got his kicks just sitting there, pulling switches and watching all those beautiful parts busy themselves functioning perfectly to accomplish nothing!

Certain sociologists saw in the machine a masterpiece of revolt against the times. But the inventor disclaimed any such intention. It was built as a mere plaything and for his own amusement. That, in itself, might be rated as a worthy purpose by some. But at best, such an elaborate layout is a rather silly and expensive toy for a man so richly endowed.

Each one of us is a marvelous creation. But we largely determine, ourselves, whether we will live purposefully, or destructively, or will merely vegetate.

Better to be cabbages than skunks or vultures. But why not be real men and real women, with the Lord's help? Such our Creator meant us to be, but he leaves in our hands the control panels of our lives, subject always to his over-all providence.

The challenge of Joshua is ours: "Choose you this day whom you will serve."

58. Situation Ethic (Religion)

Do you ever feel that you could enjoy your religion more if there were not so many rude interruptions?

This happened at our house one day recently.

I was sitting in the quietness of my study, meditating, when I was precipitately summoned to the kitchen by my wife, Maria, to face up to a real problem. In trying to chip away some of the surplus ice that had accumulated in the deep-freeze compartment of our refrigerator she had stabbed a hole in one of the Freon tubes. The Freon was spewing wildly.

In my ignorance, I gallantly took over. Imagining that we were both about to be asphyxiated, or something, I tried to stop the gas spew by holding my finger over the hole, remembering the little Dutch boy who saved his entire community from destruction by holding his finger in a hole in a dyke. But the Freon spewed on and we soon set a bowl under it and let it spew, as we scampered to fling open windows and doors.

We soon got a refrigerator repair service on the 'phone. We learned that there was no likelihood of our being conked out by the freezer gas. The problem of what to do with the contents of the freezer was solved when a neighbor volunteered to give us space in his freezer. By then it was time for me to go to church, where I had a part on the program.

When I got back to our domestic situation, an hour or two later, everything was normal again. The refrigerator firm had not only been out and picked up our ailing box for repair but had kindly installed another for our use in the interim. The only thing left for us to worry about was, how much will it cost?

Is religion something to be indulged in and enjoyed apart from what happens to us along the way? Or is real religion – like real matrimony – something relevant, "for better or for worse, for richer for poorer, in sickness or in health, until death . . ."? In the crises of life, is religion a help or a hindrance?

The religion that fails us in the hour of our need is the religion that roots in ourselves – in our "good works," in our high opinions of ourselves, in our social or economic positions. The religion that roots in Jesus Christ, the all-sufficient Saviour, is the religion adequate for every situtation.

59. Being Able to Bend (Resiliency)

Some of the comic cards you see on sale in the stores are embarrassingly appropriate. Here is one I ran onto the other day:

"NOTICE: While in this office speak in a low, soothing tone and do not disagree with me in any manner. Please be informed that when one has reached my age, noise and nonconcurrence cause gastric hyper-peristalis, hyper-secretion of the hydrochloric acid, and rubus of the gastric mucosa – and I become most unpleasant!"

Subject to the official approval of our governing boards, this might be a good notice to frame and hang just outside our office doors.

And speaking of being unpleasant, have you noticed that on the days when you are unpleasant it is also a bad day for a lot of other people too – those you run into?

Sometimes it seems that just about the time you get to feeling that you are sitting on top of the world, the world turns over!

Charley Jones says: "Trouble teaches us two things: who our friends really are, and who have been waiting to catch us bent over at just the right angle."

One of life's real tests, someone has suggested, is not how fast one travels on the freeway, but how one takes the forced detours.

And here is this inspiring suggestion from *International Altrusan*:

"Apparently it is not through strength alone that trees survive. It is not in never bending but in never failing to spring erect again, after the gale has passed, the victory is achieved. . . . Resiliency also is an important factor in triumphant living. The winds of life will bend us, but if we have resiliency of the spirit, they cannot break us. To courageously strenghten again, after our heads have been bowed by defeat, disappointment and suffering, is the supreme test of character."

Wouldn't you say that resiliency, in this sense, is one of the great attributes of the Christian?

60. Overalls Image (Respect for Persons)

Something my country friend Clabe Hankins said recently has more meaning for me after certain experiences I have just had. Clabe said in his cornbreak philosopher vein: "Most town folks ain't too powerful friendly with us fellers that wears blue denim fer dress-up."

Where I came from, a fellow was considered well dressed if he wore a clean pair of overalls and a clean, blue, cotton shirt – especially if he had most of the mud wiped off his brogans. And if the shoes and clothing were at least fairly new, he "had it made" as far as being ready to mix in polite society.

But my advice to you now is, if you like to wear blue jeans and also like to be shown some of the common courtesies, you better change clothes before you venture outside your own back yard.

And that is rather strange in this hippie-yippie day when so many people apparently could not care less about clothing or lack of it.

I made the mistake (?) of wearing one of Hankins' "suits" – blue-denim pants and loud, red-and-blue plaid shirt – to the grocery supermarket. Where I have been accustomed to kind and considerate treatment and at least a modicum of courtesy and respect, I found myself somewhat of a questionable character on the outside looking in.

Some of the clerks on whom I called for help in locating some hard-to-find items were little more than civil. And I caught one of them standing and staring at me in open-mouthed bewilderment. He seemed to be wondering, "Where in the world did this old codger come from?"

It is interesting to meditate on what constitutes the aura of respectibility in our society.

The Good Book has something to say at this point:

"If you show more respect to the well-dressed man and say to him, 'Have this best seat here,' but say to the poor man, 'Stand, or sit down here on the floor by my seat,' then you are guilty of creating distinctions among yourselves and making judgments based on evil motives. . . ." If you treat people according to their outward appearance, you are guilty of sin, and the Law condemns you as a lawbreaker. . . . Speak and act as men who will be judged by the law that sets man free" (James 2:3, 4, 9, 12, *Good News for Modern Man*).

So, do not snurl up your nose at us red necks. The Lord loves us!

61. Living for What (Retirement)

You can eat balanced meals, exercise daily, keep your weight in due bounds, and still die an untimely death just by failing to have a thrilling reason for living.

In releasing a set of "health rules" to the press, the noted heart specialist Dr. Paul Dudley White advised that there is a sense in which one should never retire regardless of how long he lives.

Said Dr. White:

"Something interesting to do will solve, I believe, half the problems of today's aging people – physical, mental, spiritual, social, and economic or financial."

Forced retirement at a given age, which is coming more and more to be the pattern of life, is not without its agony. But for those who are able to come to retirement with normal health and mental alertness, there is the challenge, in many cases, of starting whole new careers.

And the one who is in harmony with God, with himself, and with others is well adjusted and best able to adjust to the ups and downs of living – and of dying. But being well adjusted must go one step further and answer correctly the pointed question: Adjusted for what?

Whatever else happiness is – it is helping others. No activity is really worthwhile that does not include this element.

A shining example of Christian maturity and abundant living both before and after official retirement is Dr. Gaines S. Dobbins.

At age 70, Dr. Dobbins "retired" from the faculty of The Southern Baptist Theological Seminary, Louisville, Kentucky, after a long and distinguished career as teacher, writer, administrator. He had come to the point of required retirement. But he and Mrs. Dobbins promptly sold their Louisville home and moved to the campus of The Golden Gate Baptist Theological Seminary, in California, where he began what was to be a remarkable new and challenging decade as "Distinguished Professor" – ten years of teaching, writing books, and traveling and lecturing around the world.

At 80, Dr. Dobbins "retired" again and started immediately a new career as director of spiritual services for a nursing home in Birmingham, Ala. He continued to write, authoring, *Learning to Lead,* a book published by Broadman Press, Nashville.

In watching our health habits, let us not forget the urgency of being, as my country friend Clabe Hankins would say, "some account."

62. Facing the World (Self-sufficiency)

What wildlife parents do for their children by instinct, pushing them out into the world early in their lives to manage for themselves, human parents often need to do for their own offspring but all too often cannot stand to do.

Some well-meaning mothers cannot stand to discipline their children or to see fathers discipline them. By strange coincidence, these are usually the mothers who have their hearts trampled on by ugly-spirited offspring as they grow up to despise their parents more than loving them.

Just the other day one of my young friends, now the head of his own home, recalled an arrangement his father worked out for him with a farmer in another state where the young man grew up. This was the father's deal or arrangement with the farmer: "Take my son and work the shirt off him on your farm and pay him $20 per week. I will send you my check for $20 each week."

The arrangement, had the son known the details at the time, would doubtless have struck him, then a teen-ager, as a bit hard. The lad's mother may have wondered about the wisdom of it. But as the young man, now with a son of his own, looks back, he can see how wise his father really was.

One of the grave dangers in helping young people to grow up in a world that is always rather hard-boiled if not cruel is protecting them to the point of becoming over-protective. When the over-protector is the mother, we say the son or daughter is still "tied to the mother's apron string." I am not sure just what term is appropriate for an over-protective father.

Whether we like it or not, our sons and daughters come to that place in their lives where they need to "stand on their own two hind legs," looking to no one but God as they reach destiny-making decisions.

Our concern needs to be helping our sons and daughters to know and depend upon God from their earliest days and to have the right attitude of hearts to life with is ups and downs. Helping them to be self-sufficient, God-dependent Christians will be worth far more than always being on hand to tell them where they may or may not go, what they may do, what books they may read, what speakers they may hear, and so forth.

The greatest of bequests comes to us out of the last will and testament of the Lord Jesus Christ: "Peace I leave with you, my peace I give unto you: not as the world giveth, give I unto you. Let not your heart be troubled, neither let it be afraid" (John 14:27).

63. A Man's a Man (Simplicity)

Today I saw a multi-millionaire sopping pea soup with his cornbread. There are some things you just cannot improve on, regardless of your estate!

This man could have anything in the world to eat that he cared to order. And he chose to dine on black-eyed peas and cornbread! Wealth has not spoiled him. He still has his true sense of values.

People are pretty much alike, whether they are sharecroppers or financiers. We all start out in life without a rag to our backs and we go out of life with no pockets in our rags.

The only difference between a pauper and a planter is, at most, a brief period of earthly opulence. And the pauper of today may be the planter tomorrow, or vice versa. Sometimes the same person is pauper and planter the same day and at the same time.

Regardless of how much you and I are able to pile up and call ours, soon it will be gone or it will belong to somebody else. There is not much permanence in proprietorship.

Which reminds me of two young whippersnappers – nephews of mine – and some of their philosophizing I overheard just the other day. "Well," said the one who is twenty-four, "my wife and I have decided to quit pinching our pennies. After all, we can't take it with us." "That's right," said the one who is thirty-two, and who was trying to justify the expense of making another trip back home to visit relatives in Arkansas.

The all-wise God certainly must have taken the vicissitudes of life into account in making us so that our real requirements can be mighty simple when it comes to a showdown. After all, what is there better to breathe than air? better to drink than water? better to eat than cornbread and peas, with a ripe tomato and a glass of cold buttermilk thrown in, and – if you want to get real extravagant – two sizeable slices of salt pork fried well done?

Consider further our well-heeled friend who still sops his pea soup. He could have his clothes made from expensive materials from afar and by the world's most distinguished tailors. But he wears the ordinary-priced hand-me-downs, even as you and I.

Mr. Burns hit the nail square on the head:

> What though on hamely fare ye dine –
> Wear hodden grey, and all o' that –

Gi'e fools their silks and knaves their wine,
A man's a man for all o' that!

64. A Timely Warning (Sobriety)

In these days of high-pressure selling, when, according to the hawkers, one's eternal destiny may hinge on choosing the right brand of something or other, it is refreshing to run onto a series of advertisements with the indirect approach such as a series one of the major oil companies recently ran in the daily papers.

Aimed at safe and sane driving, the ads are worthy of the serious attention of everybody.

One of the ads portrayed a man with an icecap on his head, obviously trying to live through a "morning after the night before." The man was saying, "As soon as I get behind the wheel I sober up."

To this the advertiser replied, in effect, "Oh, yeah!" with the following rather startling facts:

"In a survey of fatal accidents in California, 65 per cent of the drivers who were killed had been drinking.

"In another survey of fatal accidents, in Chicago, 76 per cent of those responsible had been drinking.

"And in still another survey (they're endless), in New York, 38 per cent of the drivers who were killed had been drinking.

"Not necessarily drunk, mind you. But not sober, either.

"You don't have to feel drunk to be too drunk to drive. A single drink can dim your vision, slow your reflexes and warp your judgment. But since this alcoholic undermining doesn't announce itself with drums and bugles, you usually don't notice it. And that's what kills you: The quiet, treacherous effects of a drink or two."

Now, listen to this – and we are still quoting an oil company, not a preacher:

"A little more than a single, 2-ounce shot of whiskey in your blood can make you twice as liable to cause an accident as if you hadn't touched a drop. Two such shots of whiskey in your veins can make you six times more liable to cause an accident. (Mind you, at this level you are not considered drunk, in most states.)"

Concludes the ad:

"Contrary to popular belief, God doesn't necessarily protect fools and drunkards. And you're a fool if you think you sober up when you get behind the wheel of your car. You may sweeten your breath to fool your wife and the state troopers. And you may sit up straight behind the wheel to fool yourself. But the coroner will know you've been drinking anyway."

The time to cope with this situation is the morning and evening *before* "the morning after the night before."

65. Three Kinds of People (Soul-searching)

Here in America we are inclined to divide all people, religiously, into Protestants, Catholics, and Jews. But there is yet another trinity of division that might come even closer home to us. This is one elaborated upon by Max Merritt Morrison in his book, *Never Lose Heart.*

Dr. Morrison says, "Religiously speaking there are three kinds of people in the world." And he sets them out with no mincing of words.

First, he says, there are those who make no profession of religion and who do not make any attempt to live the religious life.

Second, are those who profess religion but do not practice it – and in this category, he reminds, are many modern church members.

Finally, there are those who not only profess their religion but practice it.

Of those who profess but do not practice their religion, Dr. Morrison says:

"Their religion promises them great things – such as power,

joy, confidence, liberty, and contentment, and greatest of all a challenge. But a great many people who have attended churches for years have none the less to confess that they have never received these great blessings."

This is due to the fact that, whatever else religion is, it is an experience, says Dr. Morrison, and many have sought it but have not found it, have asked for it but have not received it, have knocked but have never found before them an open door leading to peace and joy and assurance that life is good.

But look now with Dr. Morrison at his third group. These are the ones, he assures us, whose religion is more than a mere verbal expression of faith. For these, their religion is actually a way of life. Running through their religion is the "profound conviction that God is very near, that He is an available friend." These are the ones who say every day, if not in exact words, nevertheless in spirit: "Into Thy hands I commit my spirit."

Dr. Morrison thinks it would make quite a difference in the lives of many of us for us just to know that whatever happens to us we are still in God's hands; that even if tragedy comes, He is our strength and shield; if success comes, He is our way, He is here to save us from the corrosion of pride and to guide us and use us and our success for His glory and in the service of our fellow men.

These never forget that God never lets go of His own: "I will never leave you nor forsake you." Even in the turbulent twentieth century, these still claim the comfort that was Isaiah's: "Thou will keep him in perfect peace whose mind is stayed on thee."

66. Priming the Pump (Spirituality)

Priming the pump used to be one of the more or less regular ordeals for those of us who attended school at London, Arkansas, a generation or two ago. That was after we went modern and put in a pump, in a newly drilled well on the school grounds. Before that, we used to lie down and drink out of watering holes in the sparkling stream that ran by the edge of the school grounds.

If it had been too long since the pump had last been used, and the water that was customarily held in one of the pump chambers had leaked out or evaporated, it was necessary to have a quart or two of water to pour into the pump to prime it before it could start its flow of a fresh water supply.

Let us apply this now to another and far different situation – that of participation in the church worship services.

One of the reasons so many of us have a hard time sitting fairly still and not keeping our eyes on our wristwatches at church is that we – or the pastors – go to church a lot of the time without being primed spiritually and as a result no spiritual refreshing occurs. It is like trying to get water out of a dry pump.

Would it not be wonderful if we could get enough religion on Sunday to run us for a week? And would it not save a lot of time if we could eat and drink enough on Sunday to take care of our physical nourishment till next Sunday?

And would it not be great if one could sleep enough in a night to take care of his slumber needs for a week – and breathe enough one day to last him for several?

Or would these really be advantages?

We can be grateful, really, that the Lord used His own judgment in these matters without consulting us or even referring to a human committee.

We live one breath at a time. And most of us have two or three rather square meals a day and at least a few hours of restful sleep out of each twenty-four.

One lesson that seems to come from all of this is that no one ever gets to be self-sufficient, every one of us being dependent for every breath, every day, upon the loving providence of God, our Creator and our Redeemer. And in the spiritual realm we must look to him to "prime the pump."

The Lord maintains an ever-ready line of spiritual sustenance open to us through daily Bible study and private devotions.

67. Ground Cumbering (Stewardship)

"Why cumbereth . . . the ground?" was not asked of the Lord on a modern freeway, but on a quiet path in the Holy Land many centuries ago. If the Lord were here in the flesh today, driving a modern automobile on one of our superhighways, he might find better examples of ground cumbering in the average motor traffic than he found, even, in a fruitless fig tree.

Some of the greatest hazards to life, limb, and property in our day are to be found in drivers who either do not know how to get onto or off a freeway or could not care less. Among the most deadly drivers are the ground cumberers who stop in the access lanes leading onto superhighways and sit still till all traffic that can has passed and that which is blocked is stopped.

The bad part of cumbering the ground on the freeway is that the driver who pokes or mopes or stops compels others to cumber with him. And there is nothing any more frustrating than being forced to cumber against your will.

Sometimes the cumbering is not on the highway but in the church. A pastor who has little or no vision can be a cumberer who blocks progress for the church. Quite often the cumberer in church is not the pastor but the people. The pastor, as the undershepherd, is supposed to lead. But how can you lead those who will not be led?

According to the parable of the barren fig tree (Luke 13:6-10), when the orchardist came and found no fruit on the tree that had had plenty of time to grow up and bear fruit, he gave orders to the one who worked for him to cut it down and asked in words of strong judgment: ". . . why cumbereth it the ground?"

But the dresser of the vineyard pleaded with the owner:

"Lord, let it alone this year also, till I shall dig about it, and dung it, And if it bear fruit, well: and if not, then after that thou shalt cut it down."

Interestingly, the Lord does not tell us in the parable whether or not the owner agreed to leave the tree for one more season before cutting it down, but the implication seems to be that he did.

Certainly, one thing that seems to stand out above others is that the Lord has no place for mere cumberers of the ground in his own vineyard. But we cannot help but be gratefully aware of his unmeasurable mercy that gives so many of us not one season but many seasons to show some evidence of fruit in our lives.

68. "What Cameraman?" (Talent)

Not long ago one who was talking with me about some feature photographs he was planning to make and submit for publication asked: "What priced camera should we use in making the pictures, to be sure the pictures will be usable?"

This reminded me of the reaction I have had a few times when I have found it necessary to return, unused, photographs which were not of sufficient quality for reproduction. "But, we made the pictures with an expensive camera!" some have said in bewilderment.

It would seem obvious that the camera is only a part of the process of making photographs. There must not only be a camera, but there must be a cameraman. And, of course, there must be somebody in the photographic darkroom, developing the negatives and printing the pictures.

Even to one who knows little about the photographic processes it should be clear that the use of the most expensive camera is no assurance in itself that pictures taken by the camera will be good.

If you are going to make photographs, it is wise to have a

good camera. But, of course, a skilled cameraman can make good photographs with even the simplest, least expensive camera.

Here is the lesson this has for me. Whether one is making pictures or living a life, the thing of real importance is that the photographer or the life-liver make the best of what he has to work with. The skilled photographer can do better with a simple, box camera than a novice is likely to do with a high-priced camera with all of the latest gadgets.

And the one-talent man, or the poor, aged, sick, or afflicted man, who is humbly seeking to follow his Lord in righteous, purposeful living, will outshine the five-talent man who is worldly wise and self-seeking.

To paraphrase the late President Kennedy's, "Ask not what your country can do for you, but what you can do for your country": Do not be unduly concerned over the opportunities you have in life, but concern yourself with making the most of those opportunities. The question is not so much, what camera? as it is, what cameraman?

69. One Blown Top (Temper)

Watch that personal image!

Take, for example, what happened to a friend of mine recently. (I could find an example closer to home, but that would be too personal!)

The husband and wife had just completed their week-end grocery shopping and were being checked out. They had put into their grocery cart the "special" for the week – 29 cents worth of something or other that you could buy for nine cents provided you bought at least $5 worth (exclusive of liquor and tobacco!) and provided, further, that you had the appropriate coupon from the daily paper.

The couple was home safe on the first requirement, but the wife had left her coupon at home. "I'll bring it to you the next time I come," she promised the checker. She had done this before, but not with the same checker. The present checker, not knowing the lady, said she was sorry, but she would have to have the coupon first.

Now the husband was already pretty much irritated. Had not the checker started running the tape through the cash register before the customer had been able to place half his groceries on the counter, giving him no chance to keep up with the checking process?

"Just lay it aside," the husband said, referring to the "special" item.

Seeing that her customers were unhappy, the checker did not know what to do. So she called the store manager over and asked him, in front of a big line of other customers, if it would be all right to let the "special" go out on promise of a forthcoming coupon.

The straw that broke the camel's back was the manager's question, "How soon would you be back with the coupon?"

"I'll tell you what," said the husband, in confidential tone, "you can just have the whole outfit back." And he and his wife walked out, leaving $13 worth of groceries to be placed back on the shelves and in the freezers.

When the wife laughingly reported the experience a little later, her husband could only say, with a sheepish grin, "Hon, you talk too much!"

You and I know from past experiences how bad you feel after blowing your top. And there is not always as much involved as in this case – 20 cents!

70. Attitude of Gratitude (Thanksgiving)

Two words we focus on, as we come to observe another Thanksgiving Day – attitude and gratitude.

These are not as inseparable as "love and marriage," for they do not necessarily "go together like a horse and carriage." Every one has attitude, but too many of us fall far short on gratitude.

A little girl has illustrated this for us. When an adoring aunt gave her a dime, she held it tightly in her little fist but remained silent. "What must you say?" asked the aunt. "It's not enough!" replied the little tyke.

The little girl had attitude, but she lacked gratitude.

Let me press this a step further and ask if there is one among our readers who, looking into the past, can truthfully say, "I have never stood with the little girl, accepting a blessing without being grateful"?

Will not each one of us have to confess that there have been many times when God has blessed us and we have said in our hearts if not on our lips: "Lord, this is what I wanted, but you skimped – you didn't send enough!" Or, "Lord, you must have misunderstood! I don't want this!"

Someone has said that poverty has slain its thousands and prosperity its ten-thousands. Today we have our War on Poverty, and some of us have enlisted for the duration. But the one who reminded us that we always have the poor with us, giving us a constant opportunity to show our love by our good deeds also declared that "a man's life consisteth not in the abundance of the *things* that he possesses."

Some of us who count ourselves as far from rich have nevertheless come from poverty to plenty, to live like kings and queens, with our homes full of modern appliances that can do everything better than a host of servants.

One of the big problems of parents today is to manage somehow to get some real gratitude into their children's attitudes. Perhaps for one thing we could do as the Pilgrims used to do each Thanksgiving. Before the sumptuous meal was served, they put just five grains of corn into each plate. This was to remind that the destitution of Plymouth Colony had once been so great that the total food allotment had been five grains of corn per person per day!

How is our attitude of gratitude this Thanksgiving?

71. On Being Great (Vanity)

How would you like to receive through the mails an attractively bound book entitled *The Three Greatest Personalities of the Age and How I Met the Other Two,* with your name printed underneath as the author?

This happened to me during a Christmas season.

I got the news when I called from my house to the office to check on my mail. My secretary told me about the arrival of my "latest book" – in more than average glee, it seemed to me.

The "book" had come from a fellow editor, as a holiday stunt. I must admit that it rather jarred me. Had my friend been reading my outgoing mail – or, heaven forbid – my innermost thoughts?

Before I had brooded too much, I learned accidentally that others of my editor friend's acquaintance circle had likewise received the book, each in turn listed as the author. But not before I had done some serious introspection about my personal image.

With this experience fresh upon me I read again some of Elbert Hubbard's "Thoughts about Great Men." Said Mr. Hubbard:

"Men who do nothing and say nothing are never ridiculous. Those who hope much, believe much, and love much, make mistakes.

"Constant effort and frequent mistakes are the stepping-stones of genius.

"Men who discover continents are destined to die in chains. That is the price they pay for the privilege of sailing on, and on, and on, and on.

"The man who . . . lets his work speak, and who, when reviled, reviles not again, must be a very great and lofty soul.

"The man who can laugh at himself, and is not anxious to have the last word, is right in the suburbs of greatness."

Oh, well, who wants to be great anyhow!

72. Modern Translation (Witness)

There are lots of available Bibles and New Testaments on the market now. Most of them are written by scholars who go back to the original languages – the Greek and the Hebrew.

And many of the writers are endeavoring to give us the Scriptures in the everyday language of our times. What would the version be like that related the Scriptures to our everyday living? What would a Bible read like that showed not only what the word is according to the ancient languages, but how the word is actually translated in the lives of us ordinary, twentieth-century Christians?

"Abstain from all appearance of evil" (I Thess. 5:21).

Don't get caught.

"Therefore when thou doest thine alms, do not sound a trumpet before thee, as the hypocrites do in the synagogues and in the streets . . ." (Matt. 6:2a).

Just tell everybody about it and put it in the papers.

"Lay not up for yourselves treasures upon earth . . ." (Matt. 6:19).

Live it up on your credit cards!

"But seek ye first the Kingdom of God, and his righteousness . . ." (Matt. 6:33).

After you have your nest egg laid by in store and have torn down your barns and built bigger ones.

"Therefore all things whatsoever ye would that men should do to you, do ye even so to them . . ." (Matt. 7:12).

Treat everybody the way he treats you; be good to the ones that are good to you.

"But thou, when thou fastest . . ." (Matt. 6:17).

About the only fasting being done these days is that done by the Metrecal drinkers.

"Thou shalt not commit adultery" (Matt. 5:27b).

Except on the q.t.

"Thou shalt love thy neighbor as thyself" (Mark 12:31).
Provided, of course, that he is lovable, well-heeled, highly respected, educated, and the right color.

73. Speaking of Worry (Worry)

One of my friends was overheard chiding another for "worrying about little things that don't amount to anything."

Personally, it is the little, inconsequential things about which I enjoy worrying most. For I know in advance that even if I do not have my way about these things, it will make little or no difference. It is about the big things I rather let somebody else do the worrying.

The old Irish mother may have been wiser than funny when she said to her son who would have to cross a swollen stream on his way home one night, "Tell me exactly when you expect to cross, so that I'll know when to worry."

Those who insist on borrowing trouble can usually do so without even going next door.

Worrywarts do not get that way overnight, but over many days and nights of concentrating on potential heartaches and tragedies. It is largely a matter of the point of view and the set of one's heart.

Worry, if it is to be constructive, needs to be temporary. Like that of the young Hollander who was disappointed when his old Dutch uncle declined to give him a $5-a-week raise in wages for working in the uncle's book store. Instead of sulking, the lad promptly resigned and started his own book store. Now, many years later, he is head of a substantial book house and publishing company that bears his own name.

In most cases, worry ought to be like the changing of gears of an automobile – just a slight pause before moving into higher gear.

In time of worry, checking one's resources is a sensible

thing to do. But the greatest resources are spiritual, not material.

Freedom from worry is not necessarily absence of concern. At best it is a fearless facing of reality and walking by faith.

74. God's Presence (Worship)

For those whose five senses are properly tuned, God's presence is a constant awareness of blessing, as Helen (Mrs. S. G.) Haukedahl, of Battle Creek, Michigan, brings out in a feature of hers she has made available to me for publication:

God warms my heart when I:

See the beauty of the changing seasons – the freshness of spring, color in the fall and the soft white blankets of the winter snow, with the crystal-clear ice on the branches and the lacy patterns of frost on the windows . . .

See a fiery sunset or a full moon across a lovely lake . . .

See a beautiful mountain against a clear blue sky . . .

See the whitecaps on the ocean, smell the fresh salt air and hear the gentle lapping of the water against the shore . . .

Hear the drowsy twittering of birds just coming awake in the early morning . . .

See a beautiful building or a lovely work of art . . .

Listen to an inspiring speaker . . .

Hear the golden tones of a gifted singer . . .

Read a beautiful poem . . .

See two young lovers strolling hand in hand . . .

See the delight on the face of someone who is genuinely pleased with a gift I have selected with great care and love . . .

See the innocence of a child's face . . .

Feel the arms of someone I love holding me close . . .

Kiss the soft, warm neck of a freshly bathed baby . . .

Receive a loving look, a tender kiss, an affectionate pat from the one I love – the little things that mean so much! . . .

Gaze on a sleeping child, looking so angelic in peaceful slumber...

Hear a grandchild say, as he hugs me, "I love you, Grandma!"...

Listen to a child's prayers, with all the requests at the end for blessings for those he loves or who need help...

Feel the blessed comfort of my own prayers when my heart is sad.

75. Pen and the Bomb (Writing)

The noted Roman Juvenal said: "The incurable itch of writing possesses many."

The urge to write is a rather strange compulsion. It is hard to ignore or control on the part of those who have it. Or, as Juvenal would say: for those possessed by it. There is nothing quite to compare with the far-away look in the eye of a writer who is in labor, trying to bring forth a new idea or an old one in new garb.

The poet Keats spoke for many when he expressed "... fears that I may cease to be Before my pen has glean'd my teeming brain." Of course, some brains are more teeming than others. Sometimes the would-be writer is like the would-be speaker of whom it was said, "He appears anxious to make a speech – if only he had something to say."

G. D. Prentice said: "The Great Author of All made everything out of nothing, but many a human author makes nothing out of everything."

For those who have their moments of frustration at not being able always to come through with high quality production, W. Somerset Maugham has soothing words: "Only a mediocre writer is always at his best."

To write, to put one's thoughts in ink, is an awesome thing. It is something like walking in concrete before the concrete is dry. What is written is so permanent. And this is true quite aside from any lasting quality of ideas expressed or experiences shared. The writer must of necessity be a courageous person or somewhat of a daredevil, or a combination of both.

One thing that makes writing so awesome is the fact that one cannot write anything without revealing something of the innermost soul of the writer. For all we have to write about, really, is what we find in our own personal experiences, in our own knowledge of life and our personal reactions to the circumstances we face in daily living. Far more of us are handicapped at the point of personal experiences than because of any lack of talent at putting our experiencs on paper.

It may be that too many of us writers today are taking at face value something Mark Twain said with tongue in cheek: "Get the facts first, and you can distort 'em as you please." Books of half truth and distorted truth, especially once they get into paperback editions, often sell by the millions and poison the minds of many.

But let the writer who is honest and earnestly seeking to be a channel of truth be thankful he has been matched with the Nuclear Age. For the pen, which deals with the hearts and minds of men, is still more powerful than even the H-bomb.